Contents

Nonfiction Reading Practice Is Important

Research indicates that more than 80 percent of what people read and write is nonfiction text. Newspapers, magazines, directions on new products, application forms, and how-to manuals are just some of the types of nonfiction reading material we encounter on a daily basis. As students move through the grades, an increasing amount of time is spent reading expository text for subjects such as science and social studies. Most reading comprehension sections on state and national tests are nonfiction.

Each Unit Has...

A Teacher Resource Page

Vocabulary words for all three levels are given. The vocabulary lists include proper nouns and content-specific words, as well as other challenging words.

A Visual Aid

The visual aid represents the topic for the unit. It is intended to build interest in the topic. Reproduce the visual on an overhead transparency, or photocopy it for each student.

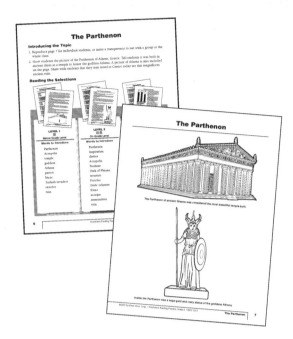

Articles at Three Reading Levels

Each unit presents three articles on the same topic. The articles progress in difficulty from easiest (Level 1) to hardest (Level 3). An icon indicates the level of the article—Level 1 (▪), Level 2 (▪ ▪), Level 3 (▪ ▪ ▪). Each article contains new vocabulary and ideas to incorporate into classroom discussion. The Level 1 article gives readers a core vocabulary and a basic understanding of the topic. More challenging vocabulary words are used as the level of the article increases. Interesting details also change or increase in the Levels 2 and 3 articles.

Level 1

Level 2

Level 3

Readability

All of the articles in this series have been edited for readability. Readability formulas, which are mathematical calculations, are considered to be one way of predicting reading ease. The Flesch-Kincaid and Fry Graph formulas were used to check for readability. These formulas count and factor in three variables: the number of words, syllables, and sentences in a passage to determine the reading level. When appropriate, proper nouns and content-specific terms were discounted in determining readability levels for the articles in this book.

Nonfiction Reading Practice, Grade 6 • EMC 3317 • ©2003 by Evan-Moor Corp.

Student Comprehension Pages

A vocabulary/comprehension page follows each article. There are five multiple-choice questions that provide practice with the types of questions that are generally used on standardized reading tests. The bonus question is intended to elicit higher-level thinking skills.

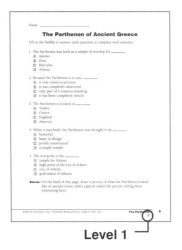

Level 1

Level 2

Level 3

Additional Resources

Six graphic organizers to extend comprehension are also included in the book. (See page 4 for suggested uses.)

Biography Sketch

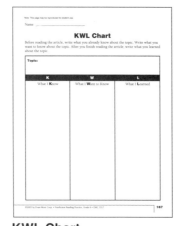

KWL Chart

Making an Outline

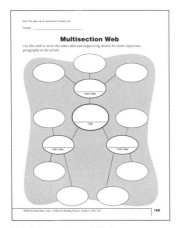

Multisection Web

Sequence Chart

Vocabulary Quilt

How to Use *Nonfiction Reading Practice*

Planning Guided Reading Instruction

The units in this book do not need to be taught in sequential order. Choose the units that align with your curriculum or with student interests.

- For whole-group instruction, introduce the unit to the total class. Provide each student with an article at the appropriate reading level. Guide students as they read the articles. You may want to have students read with partners. Then conduct a class discussion to share the different information learned.

- For small-group instruction, choose an article at the appropriate reading level for each group. The group reads the article either silently or orally and, with teacher guidance, discusses the information presented.

- The articles may also be used to assist readers in moving from less difficult to more challenging reading material. After building vocabulary and familiarity with the topic at the appropriate level, students may be able to successfully read the article at the next level of difficulty.

Presenting a Unit

1. Before reading the articles, make an overhead transparency of the visual aid or reproduce it for individual student use. Use the visual to engage student interest in the topic, present vocabulary, and build background that will aid in comprehension. This step is especially important for visual learners.

2. Present vocabulary that may be difficult to decode or understand. A list of suggested vocabulary words for each article is given on the teacher resource page. Where possible, connect these words to the visual aid.

3. Present and model several appropriate reading strategies that aid in comprehension of the expository text. You may wish to make an overhead transparency of the reading strategies checklist on page 5 or reproduce it for students to refer to as they read.

4. You may want to use one of the graphic organizers provided on pages 166–171. Make an overhead transparency, copy the organizer onto the board or chart paper, or reproduce it for students. Record information learned to help students process and organize the information.

5. Depending on the ability levels of the students, the comprehension/vocabulary pages may be completed as a group or as independent practice. It is always advantageous to share and discuss answers as a group so that students correct misconceptions. An answer key is provided at the back of this book.

Name _____

Reading Checklist

Directions: Check off the reading hints that you use to understand the story.

Before I Read

_____ I think about what I already know.

_____ I think about what I want to learn.

_____ I predict what is going to happen.

_____ I read the title for clues.

_____ I look at the pictures and read the captions for extra clues.

_____ I skim the article to read headings and words in bold or italic print.

_____ I read over the comprehension questions for the article.

While I Read

_____ I ask questions and read for answers.

_____ I reread parts that are confusing.

_____ I reread the captions under the pictures.

_____ I make mental pictures as I read.

_____ I use context clues to understand difficult words.

_____ I take notes when I am reading.

_____ I underline important key words and phrases.

After I Read

_____ I think about what I have just read.

_____ I speak, draw, and write about what I read.

_____ I confirm or change the predictions I made.

_____ I reread to find the main idea.

_____ I reread to find details.

_____ I read the notes I took as I read.

_____ I look back at the article to find answers to questions.

The Parthenon

Introducing the Topic

1. Reproduce page 7 for individual students, or make a transparency to use with a group or the whole class.

2. Show students the picture of the Parthenon in Athens, Greece. Tell students it was built in ancient times as a temple to honor the goddess Athena. A picture of Athena is also included on the page. Share with students that they may travel to Greece today and see this magnificent ancient ruin.

Reading the Selections

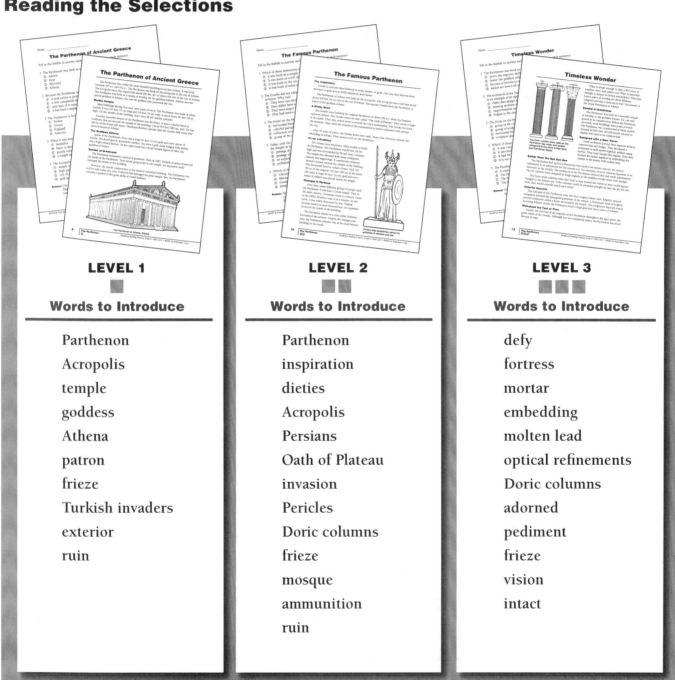

LEVEL 1	**LEVEL 2**	**LEVEL 3**
Words to Introduce	**Words to Introduce**	**Words to Introduce**
Parthenon	Parthenon	defy
Acropolis	inspiration	fortress
temple	dieties	mortar
goddess	Acropolis	embedding
Athena	Persians	molten lead
patron	Oath of Plateau	optical refinements
frieze	invasion	Doric columns
Turkish invaders	Pericles	adorned
exterior	Doric columns	pediment
ruin	frieze	frieze
	mosque	vision
	ammunition	intact
	ruin	

The Parthenon

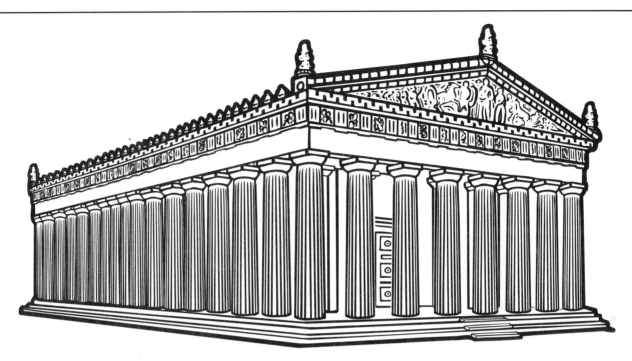

The Parthenon of ancient Greece was considered the most beautiful temple built.

Inside the Parthenon was a huge gold and ivory statue of the goddess Athena.

The Parthenon of Ancient Greece

The Parthenon was called the most beautiful building in ancient Greece. It was built between 447 B.C. and 432 B.C. The Parthenon was built on the Acropolis in the city of Athens. The Acropolis was a flat-topped hill about 200 feet (61 m) above the rest of the city of Athens. The Parthenon was built as a temple of worship for the goddess Athena. Athena was the patron goddess of Athens. She was the goddess who protected the city.

Marble Temple

Most buildings during that time were made of wood. The Parthenon was made of white marble. It was 237 feet (72 m) long and 110 feet (34 m) wide. It stood about 60 feet (18 m) high. On the outside of the building, there were 46 tall marble columns.

Another beautiful feature of the Parthenon was the frieze. It was a colorful band of sculpture that ran around the outside of the building. Out of 525 feet (160 m), only 325 feet (99 m) of the frieze still exists. The frieze showed a parade that the Greeks held every four years in honor of Athena.

The Goddess Athena

Inside the Parthenon, there was a huge 40-foot (12-m) gold and ivory statue of Athena. She stood guard, dressed for warfare. She wore a gold cloak fringed with snakes and a high-crested helmet. On her right hand was a small winged figure of Nike, the goddess of victory.

Symbol of Greatness

The Parthenon remained a symbol of greatness. Then in 1687, Turkish invaders destroyed the inside of the Parthenon. They stored gunpowder in the temple. An explosion badly damaged the inside of the building.

However, the sturdy construction of the exterior remained standing. The Parthenon can still be seen today as a ruin. Pollution has damaged the great temple. But, the Parthenon remains a symbol of the great skills of Greek builders.

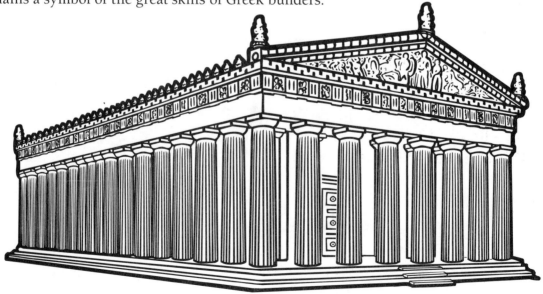

The Parthenon in Athens, Greece

Name _____

The Parthenon of Ancient Greece

Fill in the bubble to answer each question or complete each sentence.

1. The Parthenon was built as a temple of worship for _____.
   - Ⓐ Adonis
   - Ⓑ Zeus
   - Ⓒ Hercules
   - Ⓓ Athena

2. Because the Parthenon is a *ruin*, _____.
   - Ⓐ it only exists in pictures
   - Ⓑ it was completely destroyed
   - Ⓒ only part of it remains standing
   - Ⓓ it has been completely rebuilt

3. The Parthenon is located in _____.
   - Ⓐ Turkey
   - Ⓑ Greece
   - Ⓒ England
   - Ⓓ America

4. When it was built, the Parthenon was thought to be _____.
   - Ⓐ beautiful
   - Ⓑ basic in design
   - Ⓒ poorly constructed
   - Ⓓ a simple temple

5. The Acropolis is _____.
   - Ⓐ the temple for Athena
   - Ⓑ the high point of the city of Athens
   - Ⓒ the city of Athens
   - Ⓓ the gold statue of Athena

Bonus: On the back of this page, draw a picture of what the Parthenon looked like in ancient times. Add a caption under the picture telling three interesting facts.

The Famous Parthenon

The Inspiration

Greeks in ancient times believed in many deities, or gods. One way they showed their devotion to gods was to build temples in their honor.

The Parthenon in Athens was built on the Acropolis. The Acropolis was a hill that stood about 200 feet (61 m) above the city of Athens. The ancient Greeks built the Parthenon in honor of the goddess Athena.

A Shaky Start

The Greeks were building the original Parthenon in about 480 B.C. when the Persians captured Athens. The Greeks swore an oath called "The Oath of Plateau." They swore to fight to the death. They also vowed never to rebuild the city's monuments. The Greeks survived the invasion. They used the remains of the monuments to build a defensive wall around the city.

After 30 years of peace, the Greeks broke their oath. Their ruler, Pericles, ordered the rebuilding of Athens. They started work on the Parthenon.

Fit for a Goddess

The Greeks used expensive white marble to build the Parthenon. The Parthenon was 60 feet (18 m) high and was surrounded by 46 tall Doric columns. The temple was adorned with many sculptures, statues, and engravings. A continuous sculpture formed a border around the outside of the building. This horizontal band is called a frieze. Only 325 feet (99 m) of the original 525 feet (160 m) of the frieze still exist. A huge 40-foot (12-m) gold and ivory statue of Athena was placed inside the temple.

Changes in Purpose

Over time, many different groups of people used the Parthenon. It was first a Greek temple. Then in the sixth century, Christians made it a church. Later, in the 1400s, Muslims used it as a mosque. At one point, it was nearly destroyed by war. Turkish invaders used it to store ammunition. An explosion destroyed the inside of the building.

The Parthenon stands as a ruin today. Pollution has harmed the exterior. Despite the changes over time, the Parthenon remains one of the most famous buildings in the world.

Athena was sometimes called the goddess of wisdom and war.

Nonfiction Reading Practice, Grade 6 • EMC 3317 • ©2003 by Evan-Moor Corp.

Name _____

The Famous Parthenon

Fill in the bubble to answer each question or complete each sentence.

1. Which of these statements is <u>not</u> true about the Parthenon?
   - Ⓐ It was built as a temple to the goddess Athena.
   - Ⓑ It was built on a hill called the Acropolis.
   - Ⓒ It was built in the city of Sparta.
   - Ⓓ It was built of white marble.

2. The Greeks did not rebuild the Parthenon for thirty years after the Persian invasion. Why not?
   - Ⓐ They didn't want to rebuild.
   - Ⓑ They didn't have any money to rebuild.
   - Ⓒ They were angry with Athena for allowing the invasion.
   - Ⓓ They had sworn an oath not to rebuild.

3. The frieze on the Parthenon was _____.
   - Ⓐ a horizontal band of sculptures on the outside of the temple
   - Ⓑ a colorful painting that adorned the inside of the temple
   - Ⓒ a collection of statues that stood guard at the temple
   - Ⓓ a group of 46 columns

4. Today, only the ruins of the Parthenon remain. Which three things caused the temple to lie in ruins?
   - Ⓐ passage of time, an explosion, and pollution
   - Ⓑ passage of time, lack of money, and people's neglect
   - Ⓒ an explosion, a volcanic eruption, and an earthquake
   - Ⓓ pollution, rain, and wind

5. Which of the following groups never occupied the Parthenon?
   - Ⓐ Christians
   - Ⓑ Mormons
   - Ⓒ Greeks
   - Ⓓ Muslims

Bonus: You are visiting Athens, Greece, and you have just seen the Parthenon. On the back of this page, write a postcard to a friend telling about the Parthenon. Be sure to add a picture on your postcard.

Timeless Wonder

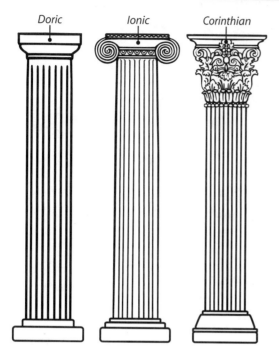

Doric   Ionic   Corinthian

The Doric column style used on the Parthenon was clean and simple, compared to the more ornate Ionic and Corinthian styles.

What is tough enough to defy 2,400 years of weather, wars, and public use? What is beautiful enough to amaze art lovers everywhere? What has been a place of worship for three different religions and also a fortress in war? The answer is the Greek Parthenon in Athens.

Symbol of Greatness

The Parthenon was built as a beautiful temple of worship to the goddess Athena. No cost was spared in its construction. Before the Parthenon was built, most buildings were made of wood. The Parthenon was constructed of white marble. Around 22,000 tons (20,000 metric tonnes) of marble was used in its construction.

Designed with a New Vision

Greek architects proved their superior skills in construction and design. They developed a technique to hold stones together without using mortar. They used clamps like staples. Then they hooked the stones together by embedding the clamps in the stones with molten lead.

Better Than the Eye Can See

The Parthenon had optical refinements that made it an artistic marvel. An optical refinement is an adjustment for the human eye. For example, vertical columns appeared to be narrower in the middle. The architects of the Parthenon realized this and made adjustments. The 46 columns were designed to bulge slightly in the middle to make them look straight.

The Doric-style columns were also built to lean toward the center so they would appear straight to the human eye. If the columns could be extended straight up into the sky for one mile, they would actually touch each other!

Colorful Accents

The columns of the Parthenon were left their original white color. Brightly painted sculptures adorned the triangular pediment of the temple. A horizontal band of brightly colored sculptures called a frieze surrounded the temple. The sculptures depicted scenes honoring Athena. Inside the Parthenon stood a huge gold and ivory statue of Athena.

Withstood the Test of Time

Finally, the survival of the majority of the Parthenon throughout the ages shows the great vision of the Greeks. Although it is not completely intact, the Parthenon has withstood the test of time.

Name _____

Timeless Wonder

Fill in the bubble to answer each question or complete each sentence.

1. The Parthenon was built to _____.
   Ⓐ prove the superior skills of Greek architects
   Ⓑ honor the goddess Athena
   Ⓒ become a fortress in war
   Ⓓ amaze art lovers all over the world

2. The architects of the Parthenon included optical refinements. Which of these is an example of an *optical refinement*?
   Ⓐ flaws that sloppy architects overlooked
   Ⓑ missing sections worn away by time and weather
   Ⓒ improvements made in modern times
   Ⓓ bulges in the middle of the columns

3. The *frieze* on the Parthenon was _____.
   Ⓐ a group of 46 columns that surrounded the temple
   Ⓑ a group of sculptures that stood inside the temple
   Ⓒ a horizontal band of sculptures depicting Athena's life
   Ⓓ a sculpture garden that beautified the grounds

4. Which of these is <u>not</u> true about the Parthenon?
   Ⓐ It was constructed mostly of wood with marble accents.
   Ⓑ It was built as a temple of worship for the goddess Athena.
   Ⓒ It had 46 Doric columns that bulged slightly in the middle.
   Ⓓ It is not completely intact today.

5. The Parthenon has withstood the test of time. What is meant by this sentence?
   Ⓐ It took a long time to build the Parthenon.
   Ⓑ The Parthenon is a work of art that tested the abilities of the architects.
   Ⓒ The Parthenon was built to last a long time and can still be seen today.
   Ⓓ The Parthenon went through many stages over a long period of time.

Bonus: On the back of this page, write a paragraph that tells why the Parthenon is considered a timeless wonder.

The United States Court System

Introducing the Topic

1. Reproduce page 15 for individual students, or make a transparency to use with a group or the whole class.

2. Read and discuss with students the diagram of how the court system works in the United States. Share with students that there are both state and federal courts. The two work in basically the same way. There is a set procedure to follow that ensures equal justice for all citizens.

Reading the Selections

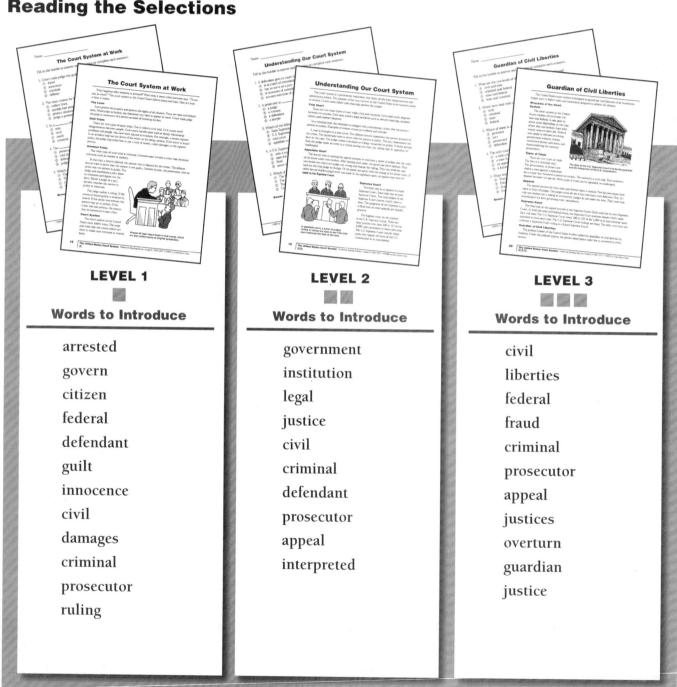

LEVEL 1

Words to Introduce

arrested

govern

citizen

federal

defendant

guilt

innocence

civil

damages

criminal

prosecutor

ruling

LEVEL 2

Words to Introduce

government

institution

legal

justice

civil

criminal

defendant

prosecutor

appeal

interpreted

LEVEL 3

Words to Introduce

civil

liberties

federal

fraud

criminal

prosecutor

appeal

justices

overturn

guardian

justice

The United States Court System's Two Levels—State and Federal

State courts handle cases that affect state laws.

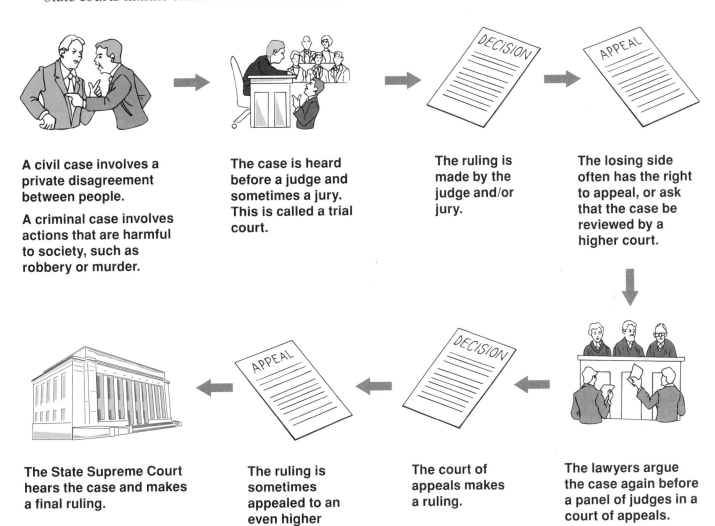

A civil case involves a private disagreement between people.

A criminal case involves actions that are harmful to society, such as robbery or murder.

The case is heard before a judge and sometimes a jury. This is called a trial court.

The ruling is made by the judge and/or jury.

The losing side often has the right to appeal, or ask that the case be reviewed by a higher court.

The State Supreme Court hears the case and makes a final ruling.

The ruling is sometimes appealed to an even higher court.

The court of appeals makes a ruling.

The lawyers argue the case again before a panel of judges in a court of appeals.

The U.S. Supreme Court is the highest court in the nation.

Federal Court System

The federal courts handle civil and criminal cases that involve such issues as federal laws, the Constitution, or when the U.S. government is one of the sides. Federal courts follow about the same procedure as the state courts. But, there are district courts, courts of appeals, and the Supreme Court of the United States. People who lose a case either in federal court of appeals or in the highest state court may appeal to the U.S. Supreme Court. The nine judges may choose to hear the case or refuse the case. Their ruling is final.

The Court System at Work

What happens after someone is arrested? What does it mean when someone says, "I'll see you in court?" The court system in the United States follows steps and rules. Here is a look at how it works.

The Laws

Laws govern the country and protect the rights of all citizens. There are state and federal laws. When a law is broken, the defendant may have to appear in court. Court trials judge the guilt or innocence of a person accused of breaking the law.

Civil Trials

There are two types of court trials. One is called a civil trial. Civil courts settle disagreements between people. Civil courts handle cases such as family relationship problems and people who have been injured in accidents. For example, a person injured in an accident may sue the driver of the other car for being careless. If the driver is found guilty, the judge may order him to pay a sum of money, called damages, to the injured person.

Criminal Trials

The other type of court trial is criminal. Criminal cases involve a crime that threatens someone, such as murder or robbery.

In the trial, a lawyer defends the person who is blamed for the crime. The defense lawyer tries to prove that the person is not guilty. Another lawyer, the prosecutor, tries to prove that the person is guilty. The judge and sometimes a jury listen to witnesses and figure out the facts. Either a judge or a jury decides whether the person is guilty or innocent.

The judge makes a ruling. If the person is found guilty, a sentence is issued. If the crime was serious, the person may go to prison. If the crime was less serious, the person may be sentenced to pay a fine.

Court System

The court system of the United States must follow rules. The steps and rules that the courts follow are there to make sure everyone is treated fairly.

Almost all legal cases begin in trial courts, which are also called courts of original jurisdiction.

Name _____

The Court System at Work

Fill in the bubble to answer each question or complete each sentence.

1. Court trials judge the guilt or _____ of a person.
   - Ⓐ fraud
   - Ⓑ innocence
   - Ⓒ criminal
   - Ⓓ defense

2. The main reason for laws is to _____.
   - Ⓐ collect fines
   - Ⓑ punish bad people
   - Ⓒ protect citizens
   - Ⓓ judge a person's innocence

3. In a _____ trial, a serious crime such as robbery has been committed.
   - Ⓐ mis-
   - Ⓑ civil
   - Ⓒ mock
   - Ⓓ criminal

4. The _____ tries to prove that the defendant is guilty.
   - Ⓐ prosecutor
   - Ⓑ trial lawyer
   - Ⓒ defense lawyer
   - Ⓓ judge

5. Which of these statements is true about criminal trials?
   - Ⓐ The judge always orders the guilty person to pay damages.
   - Ⓑ There is always a judge and jury who hear the evidence.
   - Ⓒ A crime that threatens someone, such as murder, has been committed.
   - Ⓓ The defense lawyer tries to convince people that the defendant is guilty.

Bonus: What kind of trial lawyer would you like to be—a defense lawyer or a prosecutor? On the back of this page, choose what kind of trial lawyer you would like to be and give three reasons why.

Understanding Our Court System

The court system is a government institution that helps decide legal disagreements and administers justice. The purpose of the court system in the United States is to maintain order in society. Courts must follow rules that help protect the people.

Trial Court

There are two main types of court trials: civil and criminal. Civil trials settle disputes between two parties. Civil cases involve legal problems such as divorce hearings, accident claims, and contract disputes.

In a criminal trial, the defendant is charged with committing a crime that threatens a person or society. Examples of serious crimes are robbery and murder.

A case is brought to a trial court. The defense lawyer represents the person accused of the crime. The prosecutor tries to prove that the person is guilty. The jury determines the facts in the case. The judge makes a decision or ruling—innocent or guilty. If either lawyer feels the judge made an error in a ruling during the trial, the ruling may be appealed, or challenged.

Appellate Court

The lawyer who is making the appeal attempts to convince a panel of judges that the rules of the lower court were broken. After hearing both sides, the panel has three options. They can decide the trial court judge was wrong and change the ruling. They can send the case back for the trial judge to change. Or the panel can agree with the ruling of the lower court. If either lawyer thinks a legal error was made in the appellate court, an appeal may then be made to the Supreme Court.

In appellate court, a panel of judges review or rehear the case to see if the trial court followed the laws of the land.

Supreme Court

The final step is an appeal to a state Supreme Court. Each state has its own Supreme Court. The nine judges of the Supreme Court choose which cases to hear. The judgment of the Supreme Court is final and no more appeals are usually granted.

The highest court in the country is the U.S. Supreme Court. There are nine justices who hear 100 to 125 of the 5,000 cases presented to them each year. The U.S. Supreme Court usually hears cases that require the laws of the U.S. Constitution to be interpreted.

The United States Court System Nonfiction Reading Practice, Grade 6 • EMC 3317 • ©2003 by Evan-Moor Corp.

Name _____

Understanding Our Court System

Fill in the bubble to answer each question or complete each sentence.

1. A defendant goes to court when he or she _____.
   - Ⓐ is accused of committing a crime
   - Ⓑ has to serve on a jury
   - Ⓒ is innocent of committing a crime
   - Ⓓ accuses someone of committing a crime

2. A *prosecutor* is _____.
   - Ⓐ a judge
   - Ⓑ a witness
   - Ⓒ a defendant
   - Ⓓ a lawyer

3. Which of the following steps occurs first in the court system procedure?
   - Ⓐ State Supreme Court
   - Ⓑ U.S. Supreme Court
   - Ⓒ trial court
   - Ⓓ appellate court

4. A U.S. Supreme Court ruling is _____.
   - Ⓐ only a suggestion
   - Ⓑ open for debate in lower courts
   - Ⓒ final
   - Ⓓ never wrong

5. Which of the following statements is <u>not</u> true?
   - Ⓐ The U.S. Supreme Court is the highest court in the nation.
   - Ⓑ The State Supreme Court is the same as the U.S. Supreme Court.
   - Ⓒ There are nine U.S. Supreme Court justices.
   - Ⓓ The U.S. Supreme Court interprets the laws of the U.S. Constitution.

Bonus: On the back of this page, explain how the appeal process works.

Guardian of Civil Liberties

The United States court system is designed to guard the civil liberties of all Americans. Judges have to follow rules and limitations designed to protect all citizens.

Structure of the Court System

The court system in the United States consists of two levels: the state and federal. A case goes to either court depending on the type of law that was broken. State laws mostly concern daily life. Federal laws apply to offenses involving government workers, crimes committed across state lines, and fraud involving the national government.

Types of Trials

There are two types of trials. The first is a criminal trial. The government, or prosecutor, makes a case against a defendant

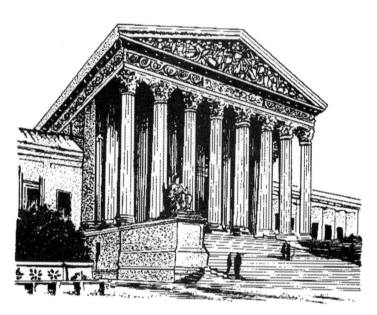

The duty of the U.S. Supreme Court is to be the guardian and the interpreter of the U.S. Constitution.

for a crime that threatens a person or society. The second is a civil trial. This involves a dispute between two parties. Both types of trials can be appealed, or challenged.

Appeals

The appeal process for both state and federal cases is similar. Two lawyers argue their cases in front of judges. The judges must decide if the trial rules were followed. Only if a rule was broken can a ruling be overturned. Judges do not make the laws. They must rule according to the laws governing court procedures.

Supreme Court

The final step in the appeal process is the Supreme Court. Each state has its own Supreme Court. At both the state and federal levels, the Supreme Court justices choose which cases they will hear. The U.S. Supreme Court hears 100 to 125 of the 5,000 civil and criminal cases appealed to them each year. The U.S. Supreme Court rulings are final. The only court that can overturn a Supreme Court ruling is a future Supreme Court.

Guardian of Civil Liberties

The judicial system of the United States is often called the guardian of civil liberties in America. Under the judicial system, the phrase *equal justice under law* is promised to every citizen.

The United States Court System Nonfiction Reading Practice, Grade 6 • EMC 3317 • ©2003 by Evan-Moor Corp.

Name _____

Guardian of Civil Liberties

Fill in the bubble to answer each question or complete each sentence.

1. What are the two levels of the court system in the United States?
   - Ⓐ civil and state
   - Ⓑ criminal and federal
   - Ⓒ state and federal
   - Ⓓ state and criminal

2. Which laws deal with crimes committed across state lines?
   - Ⓐ civil
   - Ⓑ criminal
   - Ⓒ state
   - Ⓓ federal

3. Which of these is a synonym for the word *guardian*?
   - Ⓐ protector
   - Ⓑ jury
   - Ⓒ prosecutor
   - Ⓓ defendant

4. The only court that can overturn a U.S. Supreme Court ruling is _____.
   - Ⓐ a trial court
   - Ⓑ a state Supreme Court
   - Ⓒ an appellate court
   - Ⓓ a future U.S. Supreme Court

5. What does the phrase *equal justice under law* mean?
   - Ⓐ Every citizen has a right to do anything he or she wants to do.
   - Ⓑ Every citizen has the right to be treated fairly in the court system.
   - Ⓒ Every citizen is treated the same in the United States.
   - Ⓓ Every citizen has to obey the laws.

Bonus: On the back of this page, explain why the court system is called the "guardian of civil liberties."

Queen Hatshepsut

Introducing the Topic

1. Reproduce page 23 for individual students, or make a transparency to use with a group or the whole class.

2. Show students the picture of Queen Hatshepsut of ancient Egypt. Ask students to speculate about what type of ruler the person was without revealing that Hatshepsut was a woman. Then tell students that the Egyptian pharaoh was really Queen Hatshepsut. Ask students why she would dress like a man. Explain to students that it was highly unusual for a woman to rule. She probably dressed as a man to gain respect.

Reading the Selections

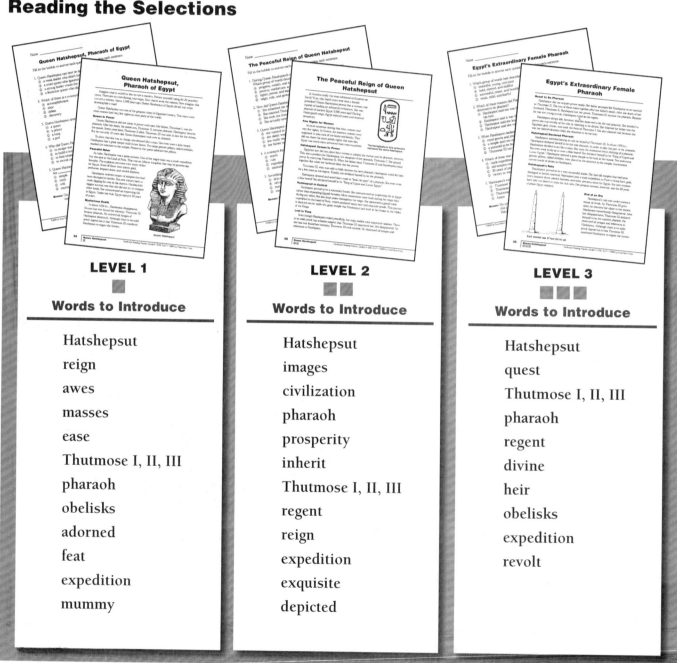

LEVEL 1
Words to Introduce

Hatshepsut

reign

awes

masses

ease

Thutmose I, II, III

pharaoh

obelisks

adorned

feat

expedition

mummy

LEVEL 2
Words to Introduce

Hatshepsut

images

civilization

pharaoh

prosperity

inherit

Thutmose I, II, III

regent

reign

expedition

exquisite

depicted

LEVEL 3
Words to Introduce

Hatshepsut

quest

Thutmose I, II, III

pharaoh

regent

divine

heir

obelisks

expedition

revolt

Queen Hatshepsut, Pharaoh of Egypt
1479–1458 B.C.*

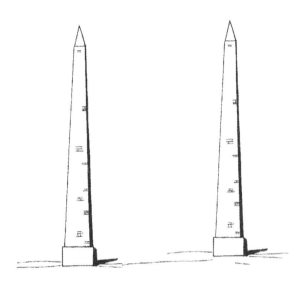

Queen Hatshepsut had a great temple and gigantic pillars called obelisks made in her honor. Stonecutters carved words of praise for Hatshepsut on the obelisks.

This cartouche represents the name Hatshepsut in hieroglyphs.

The sculpture of Queen Hatshepsut shows her in a masculine headdress. Why do you think she dressed this way?

*Dates are approximate.

Queen Hatshepsut, Pharaoh of Egypt

Imagine what it would be like to rule a country. Picture yourself ruling for 20 peaceful years. There are no wars during your reign. Your charm awes the masses. Now imagine that you are a woman. About 3,500 years ago, Queen Hatshepsut of Egypt did all this while dressing like a man!

Queen Hatshepsut was one of the greatest rulers in Egyptian history. This was a time when women had very few rights in most parts of the world.

Queen in Power

Queen Hatshepsut did not come to power with ease. Her father, Thutmose I, was the pharaoh. After his death, his oldest son, Thutmose II, became pharaoh. Hatshepsut became the queen. Seven years later, Thutmose II died. Thutmose III was next in line for the throne. But he was only 10 years old. Queen Hatshepsut took over as pharaoh.

To show that she was in charge, she dressed like a man. She even wore a false beard. Hatshepsut had a great temple built in her honor. Two large granite pillars, called obelisks, marked the entrance to the temple. Praises to the queen adorned the pillars.

Peaceful Ruler

As ruler, Hatshepsut was a great success. One of her major feats was a trade expedition that she sent to the Land of Punt. This was an African kingdom that may be present-day Somalia. The explorers returned with many riches for Egypt. Some of these were spices, gold, perfumes, leopard skins, and ostrich feathers.

Hatshepsut ordered repairs of temples that had been damaged in battles. She sent miners back to work digging for ores in the deserts. Hatshepsut's biggest success was that she did not try to conquer other lands. She concentrated on improving life in Egypt. Under her rule, Egypt enjoyed 20 years of peace.

Mysterious Death

In about 1458 B.C., Hatshepsut disappeared. No one has ever found her mummy. Thutmose III became pharaoh. He ordered all images of Hatshepsut destroyed. Although there is no solid proof, legend has it that Thutmose III murdered Hatshepsut to regain the throne.

Queen Hatshepsut

Name _____

Use your own paper!

Queen Hatshepsut, Pharaoh of Egypt

Fill in the bubble to answer each question or complete each sentence.

1. Queen Hatshepsut can best be described as _____.
   - Ⓐ a weak leader who didn't know how to rule
   - Ⓑ a cruel queen who ignored the needs of her people
   - Ⓒ a strong leader whom the people admired
   - Ⓓ a feminine queen who disliked manly duties

2. Which of these is a synonym for the word *feat*?
   - Ⓐ accomplishment
   - Ⓑ shoe
   - Ⓒ defeat
   - Ⓓ discovery

3. Queen Hatshepsut dressed like _____.
   - Ⓐ a queen
   - Ⓑ a prince
   - Ⓒ a king
   - Ⓓ a god

4. Why did Queen Hatshepsut send people to the Land of Punt?
   - Ⓐ to escape war
   - Ⓑ to build a temple for her
   - Ⓒ to find treasures
   - Ⓓ to recruit new soldiers

5. Queen Hatshepsut's death remains a mystery because no one has ever found her _____.
   - Ⓐ temple
   - Ⓑ tomb
   - Ⓒ will
   - Ⓓ mummy

Bonus: On the back of this page, write three reasons why Queen Hatshepsut was a good ruler of ancient Egypt. *★ Complete paragraph*

The Peaceful Reign of Queen Hatshepsut

Is America really the most advanced civilization on Earth? If so, why hasn't there ever been a female president? Queen Hatshepsut proved that a woman was capable of leading an advanced civilization. She was pharaoh of ancient Egypt 3,500 years ago! During Hatshepsut's reign, Egypt enjoyed peace and renewed prosperity.

Few Rights for Women

In most countries during that time, women had very few rights. In Greece, for instance, women were supposed to take care of the home and family. They did not share the same public rights that men did. Egypt was much more advanced than most countries.

The hieroglyphs in this cartouche represent the name Hatshepsut.

Hatshepsut Comes to Power

Egyptian law did not allow for a woman to inherit the throne and be pharaoh, however. This was a problem for Hatshepsut, the daughter of the pharaoh, Thutmose I. She gained power by marrying Thutmose II. When her father died, Thutmose II and Hatshepsut ruled together. But when her husband died, she lost power.

Thutmose III, who was only a child, became the new pharaoh. Hatshepsut ruled for him for a few years as his regent. Finally, she declared herself to be the pharaoh.

Hatshepsut dressed and acted like a man to "look the part" of a pharaoh. She even wore a false beard! She declared herself to be "King of Upper and Lower Egypt."

Hatshepsut in Control

Hatshepsut proved to be a successful leader. She concentrated on improving life in Egypt rather than expanding Egypt's borders. More monuments were built during her reign than during any other. She also kept peace throughout her reign. She sponsored a grand trade expedition to the Land of Punt, which produced many rare and exquisite goods. This journey is depicted on the walls of a great temple that Hatshepsut had built in her honor in the Valley of the Kings.

Lost in Time

Even though Hatshepsut ruled peacefully, her reign ended with suspected violence. There is no solid proof, but scholars suspect that Thutmose III murdered her. She disappeared. No one has ever found her mummy. Thutmose III took control. He destroyed all images and references to Hatshepsut.

Nonfiction Reading Practice, Grade 6 • EMC 3317 • ©2003 by Evan-Moor Corp.

Name _____

The Peaceful Reign of Queen Hatshepsut

Fill in the bubble to answer each question or complete each sentence.

1. During Queen Hatshepsut's reign, Egypt enjoyed peace and prosperity. Which group of words describes *prosperity*?
   Ⓐ progress, wealth, and success
   Ⓑ poverty, misfortune, and failure
   Ⓒ rights, power, and leadership
   Ⓓ reign, rule, and govern

2. How did Queen Hatshepsut finally become the pharaoh of Egypt?
   Ⓐ She inherited the throne from Thutmose I.
   Ⓑ She married Thutmose II.
   Ⓒ She took the throne from Thutmose III and declared herself pharaoh.
   Ⓓ She actually never became a pharaoh, just a queen.

3. Queen Hatshepsut dressed like a man because _____.
   Ⓐ she wanted to "look the part" of a pharaoh
   Ⓑ she didn't want anyone to know she was a woman
   Ⓒ she really wanted to be a man
   Ⓓ her father made her do it

4. A synonym for the word *reign* is _____.
   Ⓐ storm
   Ⓑ rule
   Ⓒ expedition
   Ⓓ monument

5. According to scholars, how did Hatshepsut probably die?
   Ⓐ skin disease
   Ⓑ old age
   Ⓒ suicide
   Ⓓ murder

Bonus: On the back of this page, explain why you think Queen Hatshepsut dressed like a man and wore a false beard while she was pharaoh.

Egypt's Extraordinary Female Pharaoh

Quest to Be Pharaoh

Hatshepsut did not acquire power easily. Her father arranged for Hatshepsut to be married to Thutmose II. The two of them ruled together after her father's death. After the death of her husband, Thutmose II, Hatshepsut lost her power. Thutmose III became the pharaoh. Because he was too young to rule, Hatshepsut ruled as his regent.

Hatshepsut always felt, however, that she deserved to be the real pharaoh. She decided to prove she was worthy of the title by claiming to be divine. She believed her father was the Egyptian god, Amon, who took the form of Thutmose I. She also claimed that because she was her father's favorite child, she deserved to be his heir.

Hatshepsut Declared Pharaoh

Hatshepsut resented having to rule on behalf of Thutmose III. In about 1479 B.C., Hatshepsut declared herself to be the real pharaoh. In order to play the part of the pharaoh, Hatshepsut decided to act like a man. She wore the traditional royal clothing of a pharaoh. She even went so far as to wear a fake beard! She declared herself to be "King of Upper and Lower Egypt." Hatshepsut ordered a great temple to be built in her honor. Two enormous granite pillars, called obelisks, were placed at the entrance to the temple. Stonecutters carved words of praise to Hatshepsut.

Hatshepsut's Rule

Hatshepsut proved to be a very successful leader. She had old temples that had been damaged in battles restored. Hatshepsut sent a trade expedition to Punt to bring back gold, ivory, leopard skins, ostrich feathers, and other precious items for Egypt. She sent workers back into the desert to mine for rich ores. Her greatest success, however, was the 20 years of peace Egypt enjoyed.

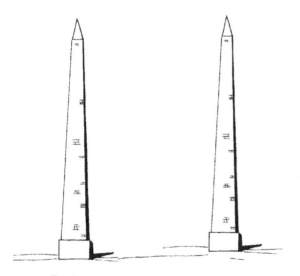

Each obelisk was 97 feet (30 m) tall.

End of an Era

Hatshepsut's rule was under constant threat of revolt. As Thutmose III grew older, he resented her claim to the throne. Hatshepsut mysteriously disappeared. After her disappearance, Thutmose III declared himself to be the rightful pharaoh. He destroyed all images and references to Hatshepsut. Although there is no solid proof, legend has it that Thutmose III murdered Hatshepsut to regain the throne.

Name _____

Egypt's Extraordinary Female Pharaoh

Fill in the bubble to answer each question or complete each sentence.

1. Which group of words best describes Hatshepsut?
   - Ⓐ beautiful, young, and kind
   - Ⓑ bold, shrewd, and skillful
   - Ⓒ successful, smart, and humble
   - Ⓓ weak, mild, and fearful

2. Which of these reasons did Hatshepsut give to convince people that she deserved to be pharaoh?
   - Ⓐ Hatshepsut said she was her father's favorite child, so she should be his heir.
   - Ⓑ Hatshepsut said it was time women were in charge.
   - Ⓒ Hatshepsut said she learned how to rule well from her husband.
   - Ⓓ Hatshepsut said she was really the god Amon.

3. When Hatshepsut declared herself pharaoh, she ordered _____.
   - Ⓐ royal gowns and jewels to be made for her
   - Ⓑ a temple and two obelisks to be built in her honor
   - Ⓒ a pyramid to be built in her honor
   - Ⓓ Thutmose III out of the country

4. Which of these was <u>not</u> one of Hatshepsut's achievements?
   - Ⓐ trade expedition to Punt
   - Ⓑ old temples restored
   - Ⓒ 20 years of peaceful rule
   - Ⓓ victory in war against Rome

5. Hatshepsut's rule was under constant threat of revolt from _____.
   - Ⓐ Thutmose I
   - Ⓑ Thutmose II
   - Ⓒ Thutmose III
   - Ⓓ Amon

Bonus: Do you think Thutmose III had Hatshepsut murdered? On the back of this page, write your opinion of what you think really happened to Hatshepsut.

The Ancient Olympics

Introducing the Topic

1. Reproduce page 31 for individual students, or make a transparency to use with a group or the whole class.

2. Have students list the kinds of sports that are held in the summer Olympics every four years. Then show students the pictures of some of the events held at the first Olympics in ancient Greece. Ask students to compare and contrast the ancient to the modern Olympics as they read the articles.

Reading the Selections

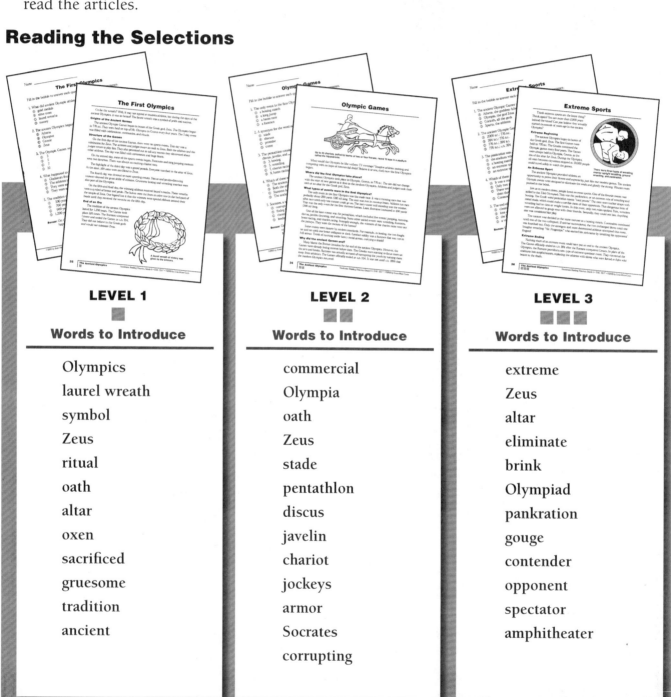

LEVEL 1

Words to Introduce

Olympics

laurel wreath

symbol

Zeus

ritual

oath

altar

oxen

sacrificed

gruesome

tradition

ancient

LEVEL 2

Words to Introduce

commercial

Olympia

oath

Zeus

stade

pentathlon

discus

javelin

chariot

jockeys

armor

Socrates

corrupting

LEVEL 3

Words to Introduce

extreme

Zeus

altar

eliminate

brink

Olympiad

pankration

gouge

contender

opponent

spectator

amphitheater

The Ancient Olympics

FOOTRACE

The footrace was called the stade. Athletes sprinted about 200 yards (180 m) up and down the length of the stadium. The runners could be disqualified if they cut in front of, tipped, or elbowed other runners.

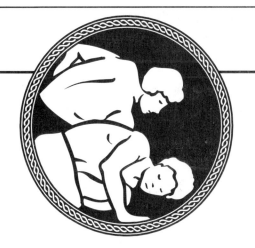

WRESTLING

Two men wrestled until one wrestler threw his opponent to the ground three times. This could take hours to achieve. The match could also end if one of the men was too injured to continue. Gouging and biting disqualified the wrestlers.

LONG JUMPING

Long jumpers carried heavy weights to give them more momentum when they took off. They jumped on a bed of smoothly raked, crumbled earth. This left clear footprints so the judges could measure the distance each man jumped. A long jumper was disqualified if he tried to inch forward once he had landed.

JAVELIN OR DISCUS THROWING

Athletes chose to throw either a javelin, which is a long pole, or a bronze discus. The athletes had to find the best throwing angle and know exactly when to let go of the javelin or discus. An athlete could be disqualified if he stepped over the starting mark when throwing.

The First Olympics

Go for the wreath? Well, it may not appeal to modern athletes, but during the days of the ancient Olympics, it was an honor! The laurel wreath was a symbol of pride and success.

Origins of the Ancient Games

The ancient Olympic Games began in honor of the Greek god, Zeus. The Olympics began in 776 B.C. They were held on top of Mt. Olympus in Greece every four years. The 5-day event was filled with celebrations, ceremonies, and rituals.

Structure of the Games

On the first day of the ancient Games, there were no sports events. This day was a celebration for Zeus. The athletes and judges swore an oath to Zeus. Both the athletes and the judges swore to play fair. They also promised not to tell any secrets they discovered about other athletes. The day was filled with ceremonies and huge feasts.

On the second day, some of the sports events began. Footraces and long jumping contests were two favorites. There was always an exciting chariot race.

The highlight of the third day was a grand parade. Everyone marched to the altar of Zeus. At the altar, 100 oxen were sacrificed to Zeus.

The fourth day was devoted to more sporting events. Discus and javelin-throwing contests showed the great skills of athletes. Gruesome boxing and wrestling matches were also part of the Olympics.

On the fifth and final day, the winning athletes received laurel wreaths. These wreaths were a symbol of honor and pride. The leaves were cut from an olive tree in the backyard of the temple of Zeus. One legend has it that the winners wore special ribbons around their heads until they received the wreaths on the fifth day.

End of an Era

The tradition of the ancient Olympics lasted for 1,200 years. The Games took place 320 times. The Romans conquered Greece and ended the Games in A.D. 394. They did not believe in the Greek gods and would not celebrate Zeus.

A laurel wreath of victory was given to the winners.

Name _____

The First Olympics

Fill in the bubble to answer each question or complete each sentence.

1. What did ancient Olympic athletes receive as awards?
   - Ⓐ gold medals
   - Ⓑ olive trees
   - Ⓒ laurel wreaths
   - Ⓓ money

2. The ancient Olympics began in honor of _____.
   - Ⓐ Athena
   - Ⓑ Olympus
   - Ⓒ Greece
   - Ⓓ Zeus

3. The Olympic Games were originally _____ days long.
   - Ⓐ 3
   - Ⓑ 5
   - Ⓒ 7
   - Ⓓ 10

4. What happened to the 100 oxen on the third day of the ancient Olympics?
   - Ⓐ Gladiators fought them in the bullpen.
   - Ⓑ The athletes ran with them through the streets.
   - Ⓒ They were sacrificed at Zeus's altar.
   - Ⓓ They were set free on Mt. Olympus.

5. The tradition of the ancient Olympics lasted for _____.
   - Ⓐ 500 years
   - Ⓑ 700 years
   - Ⓒ 900 years
   - Ⓓ 1,200 years

Bonus: On the back of this page, make a 5-day calendar. List everything that happened on each day of the ancient Olympics.

Olympic Games

Up to 40 chariots, pulled by teams of two or four horses, raced 12 laps in a stadium called the hippodrome.

What would the Olympics be like without TV coverage? Imagine athletes training and competing with no hope of commercial deals! Believe it or not, that's how the first Olympics began.

Where did the first Olympics take place?

The ancient Olympics took place in Olympia, Greece, in 776 B.C. The site did not change with the start of new games as it does in the modern Olympics. Athletes and judges took their oath at an altar for the Greek god, Zeus.

What types of events were in the first Olympics?

The only event in the first Olympics was the stade race. It was a running race that was probably about 200 yards (180 m) long. The race was run in nonstop heats. Athletes ran race after race until only one runner could go on. The last runner still standing was the winner. This was the only event for the first thirteen Games. Later, footraces increased to 400 yards (366 m) long.

One of the later events was the pentathlon, which included five events: jumping, running, discus, javelin throwing, and wrestling. Some other added events were wrestling, footraces, horse racing, and chariot racing. Strangely enough, the winners of the chariot races were not the jockeys. They were the owners of the horses!

Some events were bizarre by modern standards. For example, in boxing, the two fought on and on until one boxer collapsed or died. Another oddity was a footrace that was run in full armor. Think of running under heavy metal armor, carrying a shield!

Why did the ancient Games end?

Many blame the Roman invasion for the end of the ancient Olympics. However, the Games were already losing interest before then. The Greeks were starting to focus more on the arts and books. Socrates was actually accused of corrupting the youth by turning them away from athletics. The Games officially ended in A.D. 394. It was not until A.D. 1896 that the modern Olympics resumed.

Name _____

Olympic Games

Fill in the bubble to answer each question or complete each sentence.

1. The only event in the first Olympics was the stade, which was _____.
   - Ⓐ a boxing match
   - Ⓑ a long jump
   - Ⓒ a horse race
   - Ⓓ a footrace

2. A synonym for the word *oath* is _____.
   - Ⓐ stade
   - Ⓑ discuss
   - Ⓒ promise
   - Ⓓ curse

3. The pentathlon consisted of _____ events, including jumping, running, discus, javelin, and _____.
   - Ⓐ 3, boxing
   - Ⓑ 5, wrestling
   - Ⓒ 7, chariot racing
   - Ⓓ 9, horse racing

4. Which of these sentences is <u>not</u> true about the ancient Olympics?
   - Ⓐ The ancient Olympics always took place in Olympia, Greece.
   - Ⓑ Both the athletes and the judges took an oath at the altar of Zeus.
   - Ⓒ Runners had to wear full armor in all the footraces.
   - Ⓓ The ancient Olympics ended in 394 B.C.

5. Socrates, a teacher and philosopher, was accused of _____.
   - Ⓐ corrupting the youth
   - Ⓑ fixing boxing matches
   - Ⓒ cheating at chariot races
   - Ⓓ leading the Roman invasion

Bonus: On the back of this page, write which event you would have liked to compete in at the ancient Olympics. Be sure to give at least three reasons for your answer.

Extreme Sports

Think extreme sports are the latest thing? Think again! You are more than 2,000 years behind the times! Can you believe they actually started thousands of years ago in the ancient Olympics?

Extreme Beginning

The ancient Olympics began in honor of the Greek god, Zeus. The first Games were held in 776 B.C. The Greeks continued the Olympic games every four years. The Games were always held in Olympia, Greece, at the site of the altar for Zeus. During the Olympics, all wars between city-states stopped so 50,000 people could travel safely to watch the games.

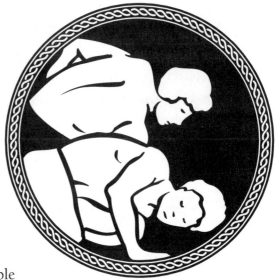

There were three types of wrestling events: upright wrestling, ground wrestling, and pankration.

An Extreme Sport

The ancient Olympics provided athletes an opportunity to prove their fitness and superiority, just like our modern games. The ancient Olympic events were designed to eliminate the weak and glorify the strong. Winners were pushed to the brink.

Just as in modern times, people loved extreme sports. One of the favorite events was added in the 33rd Olympiad. This was the pankration, or an extreme mix of wrestling and boxing. The Greek word *pankration* means "total power." The men wore leather straps with metal studs, which could make a terrible mess of their opponents. This dangerous form of wrestling had no time or weight limits. In this event, only two rules applied. First, wrestlers were not allowed to gouge eyes with their thumbs. Secondly, they could not bite. Anything else was considered fair play.

The contest was decided in the same manner as a boxing match. Contenders continued until one of the two collapsed. If neither surrendered, the two exchanged blows until one was knocked out. Only the strongest and most determined athletes attempted this event. Imagine wrestling "Mr. Fingertips," who earned his nickname by breaking his opponents' fingers!

Extreme Ending

Nothing short of an extreme event could have put an end to the ancient Olympics. The Games officially ended in A.D. 394 after the Romans conquered Greece. In place of the Olympics, the Romans provided a new type of extreme spectator event. They converted the stadiums into amphitheaters, replacing the athletes with slaves who were forced to fight wild beasts to the death.

Name _____

Extreme Sports

Fill in the bubble to answer each question or complete each sentence.

1. The ancient Olympic Games were always held in _____ to honor _____.
   - Ⓐ Athens, the goddess Athena
   - Ⓑ Olympia, the god Zeus
   - Ⓒ Corinth, all the gods
   - Ⓓ Sparta, the athletes

2. The ancient Olympic Games began in _____ and ended in _____.
   - Ⓐ 2000 B.C.; 776 B.C.
   - Ⓑ 394 B.C.; 776 B.C.
   - Ⓒ 776 B.C.; 394 B.C.
   - Ⓓ 776 B.C.; A.D. 394

3. The *pankration* was _____.
   - Ⓐ the stadium where the Games were held
   - Ⓑ a boxing match to the death
   - Ⓒ an extreme sport of wrestling
   - Ⓓ an extreme sport, which combined wrestling and boxing

4. Which of these sentences is <u>not</u> true about the sport of pankration?
   - Ⓐ It was a combination of wrestling and boxing.
   - Ⓑ Only two rules applied: no gouging or biting.
   - Ⓒ There were no weight limits, but the contest could not last for more than three hours.
   - Ⓓ Contenders boxed until one of them collapsed or was knocked out.

5. The end of the Olympics can be officially blamed on _____.
   - Ⓐ cheating
   - Ⓑ loss of interest
   - Ⓒ the Roman invasion
   - Ⓓ a violent uprising against Zeus

Bonus: Often, as many as 50,000 people came to watch the ancient Olympics. Many enjoyed watching the footraces, chariot races, and the pentathlon. But some enjoyed watching the more extreme sports. On the back of this page, write a paragraph about why you think so many people, both in ancient and modern times, seem to enjoy watching extreme sports.

No Mountain Too High

Introducing the Topic

1. Reproduce page 39 for individual students, or make a transparency to use with a group or the whole class.

2. Show students the list of accomplishments of the young athlete Erik Weihenmayer. Discuss the fact that blindness has not stopped him from being one of the top mountain climbers in the world.

Reading the Selections

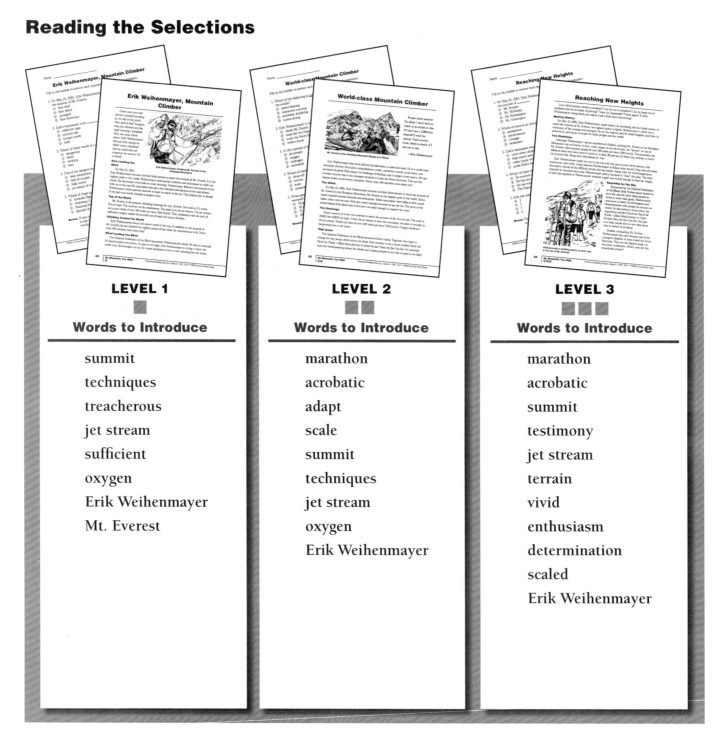

LEVEL 1

Words to Introduce

summit

techniques

treacherous

jet stream

sufficient

oxygen

Erik Weihenmayer

Mt. Everest

LEVEL 2

Words to Introduce

marathon

acrobatic

adapt

scale

summit

techniques

jet stream

oxygen

Erik Weihenmayer

LEVEL 3

Words to Introduce

marathon

acrobatic

summit

testimony

jet stream

terrain

vivid

enthusiasm

determination

scaled

Erik Weihenmayer

Erik Weihenmayer, Incredible Athlete

1968 Born with a rare eye disease.

1981 Became totally blind.

1987 Graduated from Weston High School in Connecticut; trekked 50-mile Inca Trail into Machu Picchu in Peru; named Connecticut's Most Courageous Athlete.

1991 Graduated from Boston College; trekked Pamir Mountains of Tajikistan

1993 Earned master's degree from Lesley College; crossed Batura Glacier in northern Pakistan; began teaching career in Phoenix, Arizona.

1995 Climbed Mt. McKinley in Alaska; climbed peaks of Yosemite National Park.

1996 Carried Olympic torch through Phoenix; inducted into National Wrestling Hall of Fame; received Medal of Courage; scaled El Capitan in Yosemite National Park.

1997 Climbed to summit of Mount Kilimanjaro in Africa; married Ellen at 13,000 feet (4,000 m) on Kilimanjaro.

1998 Rode a tandem bike from Hanoi to Ho Chi Minh City with his father; ran the New York Marathon.

1999 Reached summit of Argentina's Mount Aconcagua.

2001 First blind man to reach summit of Mount Everest in Asia.

2002 Became one of the youngest climbers to scale the Seven Summits.

Erik Weihenmayer, Mountain Climber

Close your eyes and picture yourself standing at the top of the world. How does it feel? Imagine that you climbed up that high wearing a blindfold. Now you must climb down. Erik Weihenmayer did just that, except he didn't wear a blindfold that he could take off whenever he wanted. He is blind!

Erik Weihenmayer climbing Mt. Everest in the Himalaya Mountains

Ears Leading the Blind

On May 25, 2001, Erik Weihenmayer became the first blind person to reach the summit of Mt. Everest. It is the highest peak in the world. Weihenmayer used special methods and techniques to make the climb. His teammates wore bells on their clothing. Weihenmayer followed the sounds of the bells up to the top. His teammates also gave him detailed descriptions of the trail ahead. Weihenmayer used a special hammer to hear the pitch of the ice. This helped him to decide if the path was sturdy enough to support him.

Top of the World

Mt. Everest is the greatest climbing challenge for any climber. The peak is 5½ miles (9 km) high. The weather can be treacherous. The peak is in the jet stream. The jet stream can cause winds of over 100 miles per hour (160 km/h). This, combined with the lack of sufficient oxygen, makes the summit out of reach for many climbers.

Climbing Around the World

Erik Weihenmayer doesn't let nature stand in his way. In addition to his summit of Mt. Everest, he has climbed the highest points of the other six continents as well. Fewer than 100 climbers have done this!

Blind Leading the Blind

The National Federation of the Blind sponsored Weihenmayer's climb. He sets an example for blind people everywhere. No goal is too high. Erik Weihenmayer is trying to show the world what blind people can do. He wants blindness to have a new meaning for the world.

 Nonfiction Reading Practice, Grade 6 • EMC 3317 • ©2003 by Evan-Moor Corp.

Name _____

Erik Weihenmayer, Mountain Climber

Fill in the bubble to answer each question or complete each sentence.

1. On May 25, 2001, Erik Weihenmayer became the _____ person to reach the summit of Mt. Everest.
   - Ⓐ first deaf
   - Ⓑ first blind
   - Ⓒ youngest
   - Ⓓ first American

2. Erik's teammates wore _____ on their clothing to help guide him.
   - Ⓐ reflective tape
   - Ⓑ scented oils
   - Ⓒ bungee cords
   - Ⓓ bells

3. Which of these words is a synonym for *treacherous*?
   - Ⓐ dangerous
   - Ⓑ blind
   - Ⓒ exciting
   - Ⓓ easy

4. One of the dangers on top of Mt. Everest is _____.
   - Ⓐ heat exhaustion
   - Ⓑ lack of oxygen
   - Ⓒ tidal waves
   - Ⓓ no means of communication

5. Which of these organizations sponsored Erik's expedition?
   - Ⓐ Juvenile Diabetes Research Foundation
   - Ⓑ American Cancer Society
   - Ⓒ National Federation of the Blind
   - Ⓓ Special Olympics

Bonus: If you could interview Erik Weihenmayer, what questions would you like to ask him? On the back of this page, write at least three questions you would ask Erik about his life as a mountain climber.

World-class Mountain Climber

Mt. Everest of the Himalaya Mountain Range is in Nepal.

People think because I'm blind, I don't have as much to be afraid of, like if I can't see a 2,000-foot drop-off I won't be scared. That's insane. Look, death is death, if I can see or not.

—Erik Weihenmayer

Erik Weihenmayer has never allowed his blindness to hold him back. He is a world-class mountain climber. He is also a long-distance cyclist, marathon runner, scuba diver, and acrobatic skydiver. Erik enjoys the challenge of finding ways to adapt to new sports. He has recently become one of the youngest climbers to scale the Seven Summits. They are the highest peaks on all seven continents. Fewer than 100 climbers have done this!

The Climb

On May 25, 2001, Erik Weihenmayer became the first blind person to reach the summit of Mt. Everest in the Himalaya Mountains. Mt. Everest is the highest peak in the world. Erik's climb required special methods and techniques. Erik's teammates wore bells so Erik could follow them with his ears. Erik also used a special hammer to tap the ice. The pitch of the sound helped Erik determine if the path was solid enough to support his steps.

The Challenge

Ninety percent of those who attempt to reach the summit of Mt. Everest fail. The peak is 29,035 feet (8,850 m) high. When the jet stream is over the mountain, the peak is actually in the jet stream. Winds can blow at over 100 miles per hour (160 km/h). Oxygen levels are dangerously low at all times.

High Goals

The National Federation of the Blind sponsored Erik's climb. Together, they hope to change the way people think about the blind. Erik recently wrote a book entitled *Touch the Top of the World: A Blind Man's Journey to Climb Farther Than the Eye Can See.* He currently tours the world speaking about his climbs and helping people to see that no goal is too high!

Name _____

World-class Mountain Climber

Fill in the bubble to answer each question or complete the sentence.

1. Which of the following is <u>not</u> one of Erik Weihenmayer's hobbies listed in the article?
   - Ⓐ speed skating
   - Ⓑ marathon running
   - Ⓒ acrobatic skydiving
   - Ⓓ scuba diving

2. Erik Weihenmayer is one of the youngest people to _____.
   - Ⓐ climb Mt. Everest
   - Ⓑ work for the National Federation of the Blind
   - Ⓒ scale the Seven Summits
   - Ⓓ write a book

3. At the summit of Mt. Everest, _____ levels are dangerously low at all times.
   - Ⓐ jet stream
   - Ⓑ oxygen
   - Ⓒ hydrogen
   - Ⓓ snowdrift

4. Which of these words is a synonym for the word *peak*?
   - Ⓐ drop-off
   - Ⓑ crevice
   - Ⓒ scale
   - Ⓓ summit

5. What percentage of climbers who attempt to reach the peak of Mt. Everest succeed?
   - Ⓐ 10 percent
   - Ⓑ 35 percent
   - Ⓒ 75 percent
   - Ⓓ 90 percent

Bonus: On the back of this page, write a paragraph describing the challenges of climbing Mt. Everest. Explain why Erik Weihenmayer's challenges were even greater than most.

Reaching New Heights

Can a blind person climb a mountain? Can he run a marathon? Can he jump out of airplanes and do acrobatic skydiving? Think it's impossible? Think again! To Erik Weihenmayer, being blind just makes it all a little more interesting!

Making History

On May 25, 2001, Erik Weihenmayer made history by becoming the first blind person to reach the summit of Mt. Everest, the highest point on Earth. Weihenmayer's climb was a testimony of his courage and strength. He set the highest goal he could imagine, and then he achieved it, setting an example for blind people and the world.

The Challenge

Although Weihenmayer was an experienced climber, tackling Mt. Everest in the Himalaya Mountains was no breeze. In fact, when caught in the jet stream, the "breeze" on top of Mt. Everest often reaches speeds of over 100 miles per hour (160 km/h). The mountain has defeated most who have tried to tackle it. In fact, 90 percent of those who attempt to reach the summit fail. Many have died along the way.

Erik Weihenmayer made his way to the top with the use of some clever devices. His teammates wore bells, which allowed Weihenmayer to follow their sound. They also provided descriptive details of the difficult terrain that lay ahead. Along with the vivid imagination required to visualize each step, Weihenmayer used a hammer to "hear" the path. The pitch of each tap signaled to Weihenmayer whether a path was sturdy enough to bear his weight.

Weihenmayer's climbing party on their way to the top of Mt. Everest.

Reaching for the Sky

Sponsored by the National Federation of the Blind, Erik Weihenmayer helped to pave the way for other blind people to strive to meet their goals. Weihenmayer continues to share his enthusiasm and determination with people all around the world. He has written a book about his experience entitled *Touch the Top of the World: A Blind Man's Journey to Climb Farther Than the Eye Can See.* His goal is to help people form a new idea about what it means to be blind.

Besides conquering Mt. Everest, Weihenmayer has now become one of the youngest climbers to have scaled the Seven Summits. They are the highest peaks on the seven continents. What's next for this remarkable athlete?

Nonfiction Reading Practice, Grade 6 • EMC 3317 • ©2003 by Evan-Moor Corp.

Name _____

Reaching New Heights

Fill in the bubble to answer each question or complete each sentence.

1. On May 25, 2001, Erik Weihenmayer became the first blind person to reach the summit of _____.
   Ⓐ Mt. Everest
   Ⓑ Mt. McKinley
   Ⓒ Mt. Kilimanjaro
   Ⓓ Mt. Aconcagua

2. Which of these is an antonym of the word *determination*?
   Ⓐ persistence
   Ⓑ perseverance
   Ⓒ courage
   Ⓓ hesitation

3. Erik's teammates wore bells to _____.
   Ⓐ warn other climbers that they were behind them
   Ⓑ help search and rescue workers find them in a storm
   Ⓒ make music while they climbed
   Ⓓ guide Erik's steps

4. Which of these sentences is <u>not</u> true about Erik Weihenmayer?
   Ⓐ He reached the summit of Mt. Everest in 2001.
   Ⓑ He has yet to scale the Seven Summits.
   Ⓒ He has written a book about his mountain climbing experiences.
   Ⓓ The National Federation of the Blind sponsored him.

5. Erik has reached the highest summits on _____ continents.
   Ⓐ 3
   Ⓑ 5
   Ⓒ 7
   Ⓓ 9

Bonus: On the back of this page, write a paragraph about how Erik's climb might inspire others to set high goals for themselves.

Ultrasound

Introducing the Topic

1. Reproduce page 47 for individual students, or make a transparency to use with a group or the whole class.

2. Ask students if it is possible to "see with sound." Actually, some animals, such as bats and dolphins, use ultrasound (the sound that is too high-pitched for humans to hear) to find things. This technique is called echolocation. Read and discuss with students the graph that shows the range of frequencies (measured in hertz) at which humans and three animals hear sound. Note that people can hear sounds that have frequencies from about 20 to 20,000 hertz. Sound with frequencies higher than 20,000 hertz is considered ultrasound.

Reading the Selections

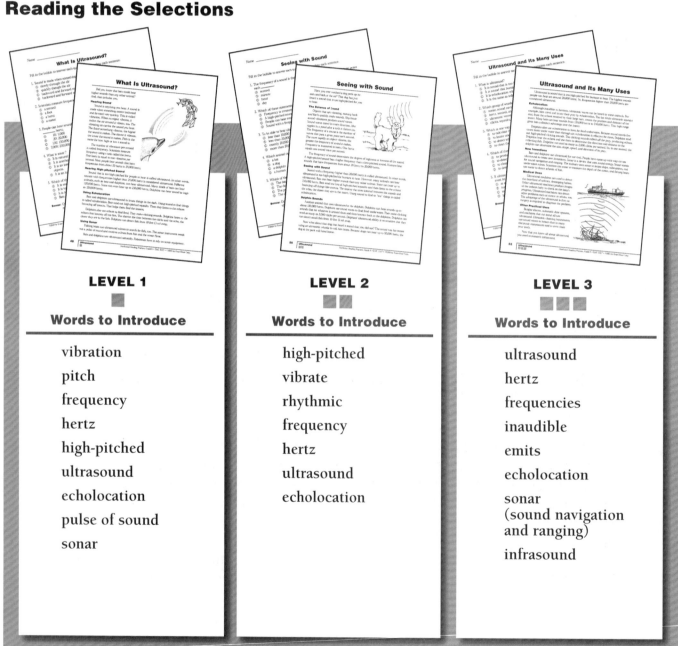

LEVEL 1

Words to Introduce

- vibration
- pitch
- frequency
- hertz
- high-pitched
- ultrasound
- echolocation
- pulse of sound
- sonar

LEVEL 2

Words to Introduce

- high-pitched
- vibrate
- rhythmic
- frequency
- hertz
- ultrasound
- echolocation

LEVEL 3

Words to Introduce

- ultrasound
- hertz
- frequencies
- inaudible
- emits
- echolocation
- sonar (sound navigation and ranging)
- infrasound

Nonfiction Reading Practice, Grade 6 • EMC 3317 • ©2003 by Evan-Moor Corp.

Common Frequency Sounds

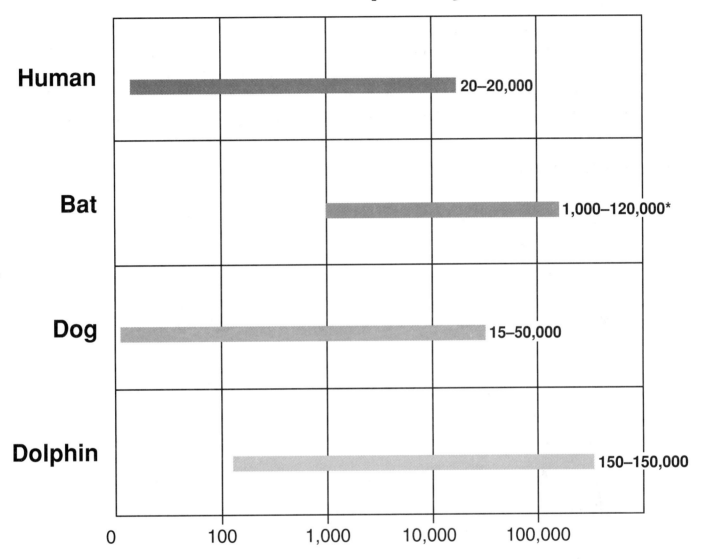

Scientists measure the frequency of sound in hertz. Frequency is the number of vibrations made by a vibrating object per second. Frequency determines pitch, which is the degree of highness or lowness of a sound. As this graph shows, humans hear sounds from a low of 20 hertz to a high of 20,000 hertz. Any frequency above 20,000 hertz is considered ultrasound, or too high-pitched for a human.

*Note: These ranges are approximate. Some species of bats can hear up to 210,000 hertz.

What Is Ultrasound?

Did you know that bats could hear higher sounds than any other animal? And, that includes you.

Hearing Sound

Sound is anything you hear. A sound is made when something moves backward and forward very quickly. This is called vibration. When an object vibrates, it makes the air around it vibrate, too. The vibrating air carries the sound you hear. The faster something vibrates, the higher the sound it makes. The slower it vibrates, the lower the sound it makes. *Pitch* is the name for how high or low a sound is.

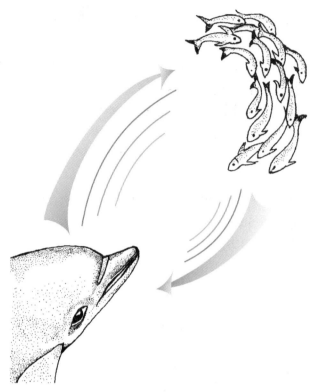

The number of vibrations per second is called frequency. Scientists measure frequency using a unit called the hertz. One hertz is equal to one vibration per second. Most people hear sounds that have frequencies from about 20 hertz to 20,000 hertz.

Hearing High-pitched Sound

Sound that is too high-pitched for people to hear is called ultrasound. In other words, sounds with frequencies higher than 20,000 hertz is considered ultrasound. Different animals, such as bats and dolphins, can hear ultrasound. Many kinds of bats can hear 120,000 hertz. Some can even hear up to 210,000 hertz. Dolphins can hear sound as high as 150,000 hertz.

Using Echolocation

Bats and dolphins use ultrasound to locate things in the dark. Using sound to find things is called echolocation. Bats send out high-pitched squeaks. Then they listen to the echoes bouncing off insects. That helps them find the insects.

Dolphins also use echoes to find food. They make clicking sounds. Dolphins listen to the echoes that bounce off the fish. The shorter the time between the clicks and the echo, the closer they are to the fish. Dolphins can detect fish from 10 feet (3 m) away.

Using Sonar

Fishing boats use ultrasound echoes to search for fish, too. The sonar instrument sends out a pulse of sound and receives echoes from fish and the ocean floor.

Bats and dolphins use ultrasound naturally. Fishermen have to rely on sonar equipment.

Name _____

What Is Ultrasound?

Fill in the bubble to answer each question or complete each sentence.

1. Sound is made when something vibrates, or moves _____.
   Ⓐ slowly through the air
   Ⓑ quickly though the air
   Ⓒ backward and forward very slowly
   Ⓓ backward and forward very quickly

2. Scientists measure frequency using the unit called _____.
   Ⓐ a second
   Ⓑ a foot
   Ⓒ a hertz
   Ⓓ a meter

3. People can hear sounds that have frequencies from about _____ to
   _____ hertz.
   Ⓐ   10; 1,000
   Ⓑ   20; 20,000
   Ⓒ   150; 150,000
   Ⓓ 7,000; 210,000

4. What is *sonar*?
   Ⓐ It is natural sound coming from the ocean floor.
   Ⓑ It is another word for the frequency of sound.
   Ⓒ It is an instrument that uses sounds and echoes to locate underwater
      objects.
   Ⓓ It is an instrument that helps keep dolphins away from the fishing boats.

5. Which of these statements is <u>not</u> true about ultrasound?
   Ⓐ It is sound with a frequency higher than 20,000 hertz.
   Ⓑ It is too low-pitched for humans to hear.
   Ⓒ It is too high-pitched for humans to hear.
   Ⓓ Bats and dolphins use ultrasound to locate food.

Bonus: On the back of this page, draw a diagram of how a dolphin uses
echolocation. Be sure to label the diagram and include a caption.

Seeing with Sound

Have you ever watched a dog perk up its ears and bark at the air? That dog has just heard a sound that is too high-pitched for you to hear.

The Science of Sound

Objects that are vibrating, moving back and forth quickly, make sounds. Rhythmic sound vibrations produce sound waves. Sound waves travel in every direction, like ripples in a pond after a rock is thrown in. The frequency of a sound is the number of waves that pass a given point each second. The more rapidly an object vibrates, the greater the frequency of sound it makes. Frequency is measured in hertz. One hertz equals one sound wave per second.

The frequency of sound determines the degree of highness or lowness of the sound. A high-pitched sound has a higher frequency than a low-pitched sound. Humans hear sounds that have frequencies from about 20 hertz to 20,000 hertz.

Seeing with Sound

Sound with a frequency higher than 20,000 hertz is called ultrasound. In other words, ultrasound is too high-pitched for humans to hear. However, many animals can hear ultrasound. Bats can hear higher sounds than any other animal. Some can hear up to 210,000 hertz. Bats send out lots of high-pitched squeaks and then listen to the echoes bouncing off things like insects. The shorter the time interval between the squeak and the echo, the closer they are to the insect. Using sound to find or "see" things is called echolocation.

Dolphin Sounds

Another animal that uses ultrasound is the dolphin. Dolphins can hear sounds up to about 150,000 hertz. Dolphins use sound waves to find food underwater. They make clicking sounds that hit whatever is around them and then bounce back to the dolphins. Dolphins can send as many as 2,000 clicks per second. Dolphins' ultrasound ability is so sensitive that they can detect small fish from 10 feet (3 m) away.

Now what about that dog that heard a sound that you did not? The sound was his owner using an ultrasonic whistle to call him home. Because dogs can hear up to 50,000 hertz, the dog at the park will head home.

Nonfiction Reading Practice, Grade 6 • EMC 3317 • ©2003 by Evan-Moor Corp.

Name _____

Seeing with Sound

Fill in the bubble to answer each question or complete each sentence.

1. The frequency of a sound is the number of sound waves that pass a given point each _____.
   Ⓐ second
   Ⓑ minute
   Ⓒ hour
   Ⓓ day

2. Which of these statements is true about the frequency of sound?
   Ⓐ Frequency is measured in hertz per minute.
   Ⓑ A high-pitched sound has a lower frequency than a low-pitched sound.
   Ⓒ People can hear sounds that have frequencies up to 20,000 hertz.
   Ⓓ Sound with a frequency higher than 20,000 hertz is called vibration.

3. To be able to hear ultrasound, you must be able to hear _____.
   Ⓐ less than 10,000 hertz
   Ⓑ less than 20,000 hertz
   Ⓒ exactly 20,000 hertz
   Ⓓ more than 20,000 hertz

4. Which animal can hear the highest ultrasound?
   Ⓐ a bat
   Ⓑ a dog
   Ⓒ a dolphin
   Ⓓ a human

5. Which of these statements is an example of *echolocation*?
   Ⓐ The bat caught the insect in midair and flew off to eat it.
   Ⓑ The dolphin made clicking sounds that bounced off the fish and back to it.
   Ⓒ The person heard an echo when he shouted into the canyon.
   Ⓓ The dog heard his owner's ultrasonic whistle because he used ultrasound.

Bonus: On the back of this page, write a definition for the following words: *vibration, frequency, hertz, ultrasound,* and *echolocation.*

Ultrasound and Its Many Uses

Ultrasound is sound that is too high-pitched for humans to hear. The highest sounds people can hear are around 20,000 hertz. So, frequencies higher than 20,000 hertz are considered ultrasound.

Echolocation

Although inaudible to humans, ultrasonic waves can be heard by some animals. For example, bats travel and locate their prey by echolocation. The bat emits ultrasonic squeaks and, from the echoes received by their large ears, senses the position and distance of the insect. Many bats can hear sounds from 120,000 hertz to 210,000 hertz. This high range gives bats a distinct advantage over the insect.

Dolphins also use echolocation to hunt for food underwater. Because sound travels five times faster under water than through air, echolocation is effective for them. Dolphins send out high-pitched clicking sounds. The clicking sounds reflect off the prey, producing echoes. Dolphins hear the echoes and use them to determine the direction and distance to the reflecting fish. Dolphins can send as many as 2,000 clicks per second. So, in one second, the dolphin can determine the size, shape, speed, and direction of its prey.

New Inventions

Bats and dolphins use ultrasound for survival. People have come up with ways to use ultrasound to create new inventions. Sonar is a device that uses sound energy. Sonar stands for sound navigation and ranging. The military uses sonar to locate ships, submarines, and underwater mines. Scientists use sonar to measure the depth of the ocean, and fishing boats use sonar to detect schools of fish.

Medical Uses

Ultrasound machines are used to detect the heartbeat of unborn, developing babies. Other ultrasound machines produce images of the unborn baby to check on the baby's progress. Ultrasound machines can detect other problems such as cancer in adults, too. The advantage of the ultrasound is that no surgery is required to diagnose the problem.

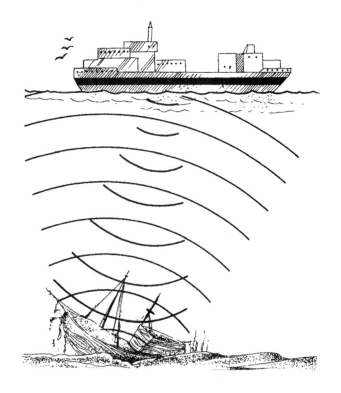

Other Practical Uses

Burglar alarms, automatic door openers, and machines that cut metal all use ultrasound. Ultrasonic cleaning instruments use sound waves to loosen dust in many electronic components and to even clean your teeth.

Now that you know all about ultrasound, you need to research infrasound.

Name _____

Ultrasound and Its Many Uses

Fill in the bubble to answer each question or complete each sentence.

1. What is *ultrasound*?
   - Ⓐ It is sound that is too high-pitched for humans to hear.
   - Ⓑ It is sound that humans, bats, and dolphins hear.
   - Ⓒ It is echolocation without sonar.
   - Ⓓ It is the same as infrasound.

2. Which group of words best describes the term *echolocation*?
   - Ⓐ sonar, sound navigation, and ranging
   - Ⓑ hertz, second, and distance
   - Ⓒ ultrasonic waves, echoes, and reflection
   - Ⓓ clicks, squeaks, and high-pitched sounds

3. Which is one way the military uses sonar devices?
   - Ⓐ to calculate the depth of the ocean
   - Ⓑ to locate underwater mines
   - Ⓒ to detect schools of fish
   - Ⓓ to clean the electronic components aboard ships

4. Which of these uses for ultrasound was <u>not</u> mentioned in the article?
   - Ⓐ to produce images of unborn, developing babies
   - Ⓑ to detect cancer and other diseases
   - Ⓒ to clean instruments and teeth
   - Ⓓ to detect flaws in metal parts

5. If ultrasound is sound that is too high-pitched for humans to hear, *infrasound* must be _____.
   - Ⓐ at a pitch that humans can hear
   - Ⓑ too low-pitched for humans to hear
   - Ⓒ too many sounds that blend together
   - Ⓓ inaudible to any animals

Bonus: Navy ships use sonar along the migratory routes of whales. Ultrasonic waves seem to disorient the whales. Environmentalists want the navy to stop using sonar along this route. The navy says it must use sonar to protect our coastline from threats of terrorism. On the back of this page, write your opinion about this problem and include any solutions you think would solve this dilemma.

Manatees

Introducing the Topic

1. Reproduce page 55 for individual students, or make a transparency to use with a group or the whole class.

2. Show students the picture of the manatee. Discuss with students that there are three different species of manatees. Manatees can be found in Africa, South America, and the southeastern coast of the United States. Share with students that manatees are an endangered species. They will read to find out facts about manatees and learn about the dangers facing these gentle giants of the sea.

Reading the Selections

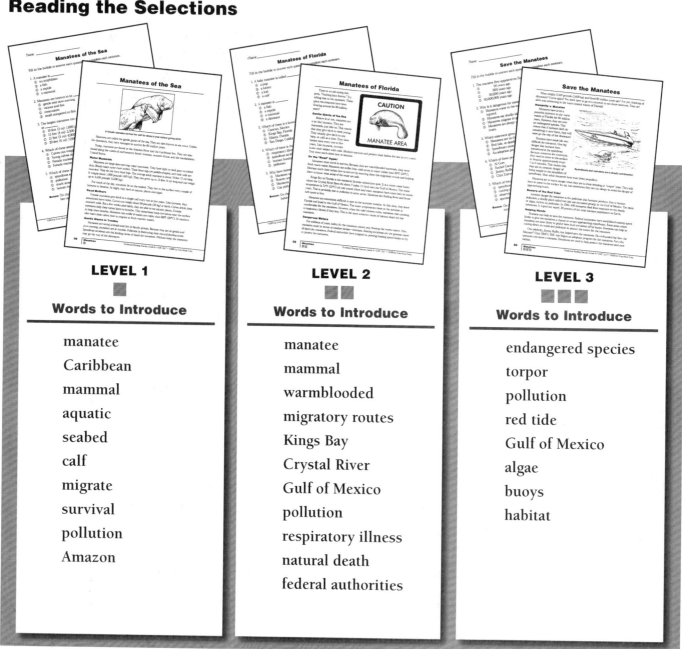

LEVEL 1
Words to Introduce

- manatee
- Caribbean
- mammal
- aquatic
- seabed
- calf
- migrate
- survival
- pollution
- Amazon

LEVEL 2
Words to Introduce

- manatee
- mammal
- warmblooded
- migratory routes
- Kings Bay
- Crystal River
- Gulf of Mexico
- pollution
- respiratory illness
- natural death
- federal authorities

LEVEL 3
Words to Introduce

- endangered species
- torpor
- pollution
- red tide
- Gulf of Mexico
- algae
- buoys
- habitat

Manatees

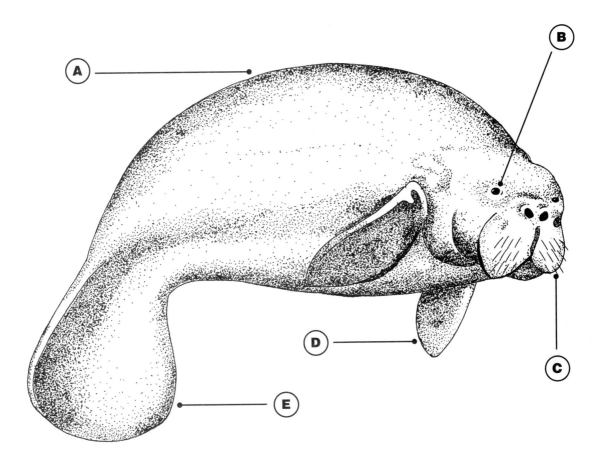

Manatees are huge, gentle, and slow-moving water mammals. They may grow up to 13 feet (4 m) long and weigh up to 3,500 pounds (1,600 kg).

A Bristly hairs cover their gray wrinkled skin.

B Two very small eyes help them to see fairly well.

C They have thick whiskers on their snouts and their upper lip is divided into halves. The halves give manatees a good grip on the plants they eat.

D Front flippers are paddle-shaped and used for steering and scooping up food. Three to four nails are on each flipper.

E The paddle-shaped tail moves their bodies through the water.

Manatees of the Sea

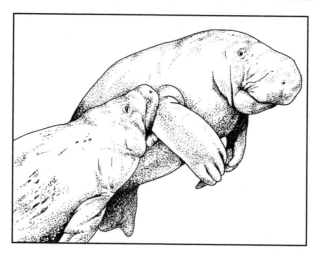

A female manatee carries her calf for about a year before giving birth.

Manatees are called the gentle giants of the sea. They are also known as sea cows. Unlike the dinosaurs, they have managed to survive for 60 million years.

Today, manatees are found in the Amazon River and the Caribbean Sea. They are also found along the coasts of northeastern South America, western Africa, and the southeastern United States.

Water Mammals

Manatees are large slow-moving water mammals. They have light to dark gray wrinkled skin. Bristly hairs cover their bodies. Their front legs are paddle-shaped, and their tails are rounded. They do not have hind legs. The average adult manatee is about 10 feet (3 m) long. It weighs about 1,000 pounds (450 kg). They can grow up to 13 feet (4 m) long and can weigh up to 3,500 pounds (1,600 kg).

For much of the day, manatees lie on the seabed. They rise to the surface every couple of minutes to breathe. At night, they feed on aquatic plants and algae.

Good Mothers

Female manatees give birth to a single calf every two to five years. Like humans, they sometimes have twins. Calves can weigh about 60 pounds (30 kg) at birth. Calves drink their mother's milk. But a few weeks after birth, they are able to eat aquatic plants. Female manatees help their calves learn to breathe. They sometimes keep the calves near the surface to help them breathe. Manatees can suffer if waters are colder than 68°F (20°C). So mothers also teach their calves how to migrate to fresh warmer waters.

Gentle Giants in Trouble

Manatees are social animals and live in family groups. Because they are so gentle and slow-moving, manatees are in trouble. Pollution is destroying their natural feeding areas. Speedboat accidents are the leading cause of death for manatees. Without help, the manatees may go the way of the dinosaurs.

Name _____

Manatees of the Sea

Fill in the bubble to answer each question or complete each sentence.

1. A *manatee* is _____.
   - Ⓐ an amphibian
   - Ⓑ a fish
   - Ⓒ a reptile
   - Ⓓ a mammal

2. Manatees are known to be _____.
   - Ⓐ gentle and slow-moving
   - Ⓑ vicious and fast
   - Ⓒ meat-eaters
   - Ⓓ small compared to fish

3. The largest manatees can grow up to _____ long and weigh as much as _____.
   - Ⓐ 10 feet (3 m); 1,000 pounds (450 kg)
   - Ⓑ 13 feet (4 m); 3,500 pounds (1,600 kg)
   - Ⓒ 15 feet (5 m); 4,000 pounds (1,800 kg)
   - Ⓓ 20 feet (6 m); 5,000 pounds (2,250 kg)

4. Which of these sentences is not true about manatee calves?
   - Ⓐ Calves can weigh about 60 pounds (30 kg) at birth.
   - Ⓑ Young calves drink their mother's milk.
   - Ⓒ Female manatees can give birth to only one calf.
   - Ⓓ Female manatees teach their calves how to surface to breathe.

5. Which of these is the leading cause of death for manatees?
   - Ⓐ speedboat accidents
   - Ⓑ pollution
   - Ⓒ shark attacks
   - Ⓓ human hunting

Bonus: On the back of this page, explain how a manatee mother helps prepare her calf for survival.

Manatees of Florida

There is an old saying that goes, "Nothing lasts forever." Try telling that to the manatees. These giant sea creatures have been floating around for 60 million years!

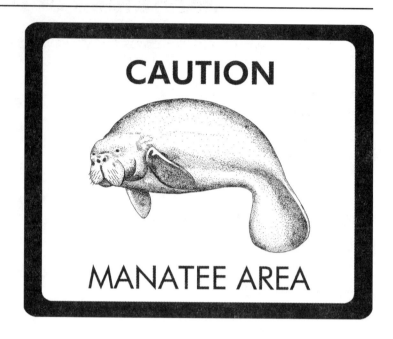

Gentle Giants of the Sea

Believe it or not, manatees are a lot like humans. They are mammals, just like us. This means that they give birth to their young. They usually give birth to one baby, or calf, at a time. They have babies once every two to five years. Like humans, mothers nurse their babies with milk. Mothers nurture and protect their babies for one to two years. They even teach them how to breathe.

On the "Road" Again!

Manatees must travel to survive. Because they are warmblooded mammals, they need fresh warm water. Manatees can suffer from cold stress in water colder than 68°F (20°C). Mothers teach their babies how to survive by showing them the migratory routes and helping them to know what areas of the water are safe.

Kings Bay in Florida is the manatees' favorite wintertime spot. It is a warm water basin where the Crystal River flows for about 7 miles (11 km) into the Gulf of Mexico. The water temperature is 72°F (22°C) all year round. More and more manatees have come here in recent years. This is probably due to pollution in other areas. Manatees are finding fewer and fewer safe spots to live.

Manatees are sometimes difficult to spot in the summer months. At this time, they leave Florida and head to the Gulf of Mexico. The water temperature there in the summer is comfortable for the manatees. However, when the cold winters come, manatees risk catching a respiratory illness if they stay. This is the most common cause of natural death for the manatees.

Dangerous Waters

For millions of years, safety for the manatees meant only finding the warm waters. Now, manatees must be aware of another danger—humans. Boating accidents are the greatest cause of death for manatees. Federal authorities have stepped in, posting boating speed limits to try to protect the manatees.

Nonfiction Reading Practice, Grade 6 • EMC 3317 • ©2003 by Evan-Moor Corp.

Manatees of Florida

Fill in the bubble to answer each question or complete each sentence.

1. A *baby manatee* is called _____.
   - Ⓐ a pup
   - Ⓑ a kitten
   - Ⓒ a kid
   - Ⓓ a calf

2. A *manatee* is _____.
   - Ⓐ a fish
   - Ⓑ a reptile
   - Ⓒ a mammal
   - Ⓓ a dinosaur

3. Which of these is a favorite migratory spot of the manatees?
   - Ⓐ Cancun, Mexico
   - Ⓑ Kings Bay, Florida
   - Ⓒ Miami, Florida
   - Ⓓ San Diego, California

4. Which of these is the most common natural death of the manatees?
   - Ⓐ respiratory illness
   - Ⓑ speedboat accidents
   - Ⓒ human hunting
   - Ⓓ pollution

5. Why have federal authorities posted boating speed limits?
   - Ⓐ Manatees are becoming too populated.
   - Ⓑ Boaters are afraid of manatees.
   - Ⓒ Manatees are in danger of extinction because of boating accidents.
   - Ⓓ Gas pollution from boats is stronger at high speeds.

Bonus: On the back of this page, write a paragraph explaining the migratory habits of manatees.

Save the Manatees

What weighs 3,500 pounds (1,600 kg) and lived 60 million years ago? Are you thinking of dinosaurs? Guess again! You don't have to go to a museum to see these creatures. They are alive and swimming in the warm coastal waters of Florida!

Humanity v. Manatee

Manatees have lived a peaceful existence in the warm waters of Florida for 60 million years. However, they are now an endangered species. This means that if humans don't do something to save them, they will soon go the way of the dinosaurs!

Humans have made life very difficult for manatees. One big danger that humans have introduced is the speedboat. Because manatees are mammals, they need to come to the surface to breathe approximately every 5 to 6 minutes. This means that they are in constant danger of being caught in the propellers of speedboats. Most adult manatees have scars from propellers.

Speedboats and manatees are a deadly combination.

Manatees are in extra danger when they are in their sleeping or "torpor" state. They still have to come to the surface for air, but sometimes they are too sleepy to avoid the danger of approaching boats.

Beware of the Red Tide!

Another danger for manatees is the pollution that humans produce. Due to human pollution, a deadly plant called red tide has increased greatly in the Gulf of Mexico. The plant, or algae, thrives on pollution. In 1996, 400 manatees died from exposure to the deadly substance. It wiped out nearly 20 percent of the total manatee population on Earth.

Helping Hands

Humans can help to save the manatees. Federal authorities have established boating speed limits to give the manatees a chance to escape approaching speedboats. Some areas where manatees are most likely to gather have been sectioned off by buoys. Everyone can help by cutting down on waste and pollution to protect the waters for the manatees.

One celebrity, Jimmy Buffet, has helped save the manatees. He co-founded the Save the Manatee® Club (SMC). SMC has begun an adoption program for the manatees. For a fee, sponsors can name a manatee. Donations are used to help protect the manatees and their habitat.

Nonfiction Reading Practice, Grade 6 • EMC 3317 • ©2003 by Evan-Moor Corp.

Name _____

Save the Manatees

Fill in the bubble to answer each question or complete each sentence.

1. The manatee first appeared on Earth about _____.
   Ⓐ   60 years ago
   Ⓑ   600 years ago
   Ⓒ   60,000 years ago
   Ⓓ 60,000,000 years ago

2. Why is it dangerous for manatees to be in a torpor state?
   Ⓐ Manatees come to the surface to breathe, and that is when they are injured.
   Ⓑ Manatees eat deadly algae, and this makes them too sick to avoid danger.
   Ⓒ Manatees migrate in groups, so they are easily hurt by passing boats.
   Ⓓ Manatees are sleepy when they surface, so they can't avoid approaching boats.

3. Which statement gives a cause for why manatees are endangered?
   Ⓐ Manatees are in the most danger when they are in a torpor state.
   Ⓑ Red tide, or deadly algae, is polluting the Gulf of Mexico.
   Ⓒ Speedboats must obey speed limits.
   Ⓓ An adoption program to save the manatees has helped them.

4. Which of these people co-founded the Save the Manatees Club?
   Ⓐ Al Gore
   Ⓑ Rachel Carson
   Ⓒ Jimmy Buffet
   Ⓓ Clint Eastwood

5. Which of these is <u>not</u> a way to help save the manatees?
   Ⓐ speedboat racing
   Ⓑ cutting down on waste and pollution
   Ⓒ observing boating speed limits
   Ⓓ sponsoring a manatee by making a donation

Bonus: On the back of this page, write a paragraph explaining what humans can do to help save the manatees.

Apollo 13

Introducing the Topic

1. Reproduce page 63 for individual students, or make a transparency to use with a group or the whole class.

2. Ask students if they have ever heard what happened on the Apollo 13 mission to the moon. Show students the picture of the two spacecrafts. Explain to students that the *Odyssey* was the Command and Service Module. Tell them the other craft is the Lunar Module, *Aquarius*. Explain that *Aquarius*, originally meant to help the crew land on the moon, actually helped save their lives.

Reading the Selections

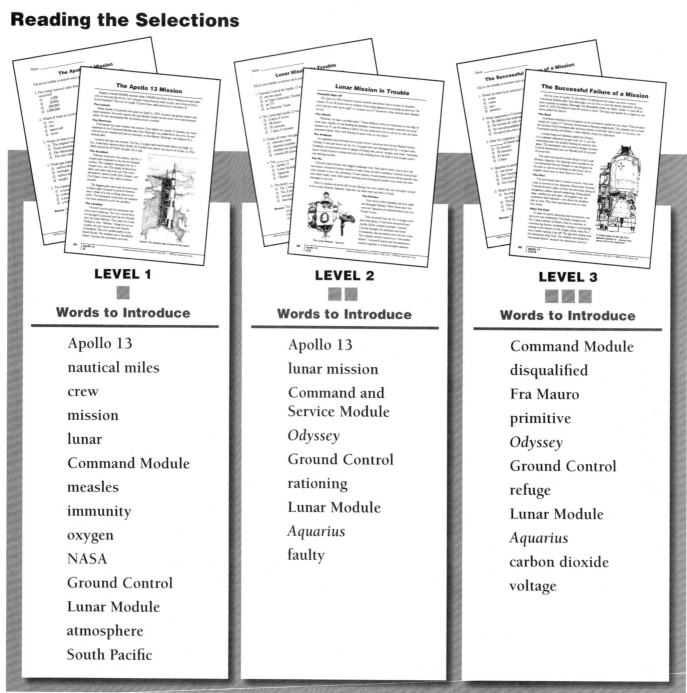

LEVEL 1

Words to Introduce

Apollo 13
nautical miles
crew
mission
lunar
Command Module
measles
immunity
oxygen
NASA
Ground Control
Lunar Module
atmosphere
South Pacific

LEVEL 2

Words to Introduce

Apollo 13
lunar mission
Command and Service Module
Odyssey
Ground Control
rationing
Lunar Module
Aquarius
faulty

LEVEL 3

Words to Introduce

Command Module
disqualified
Fra Mauro
primitive
Odyssey
Ground Control
refuge
Lunar Module
Aquarius
carbon dioxide
voltage

The Apollo 13 Mission to the Moon

Odyssey,
the Command Module

Aquarius,
the Lunar Module

The launch took place on April 11, 1970. Astronauts James Lovell, John Swigert, and Fred Haise were to explore the Fra Mauro region on the moon. Fifty-six hours into the flight, an explosion on the *Odyssey* turned this lunar mission into a terrifying and heroic rescue mission instead.

The Apollo 13 Mission

Imagine yourself 200,000 nautical miles (370,400 km) from Earth floating through space with no real plan for return. Now imagine being freezing cold, hungry, and dying of thirst. Sound hopeless? The crew of Apollo 13 faced these odds and lived to tell about it!

The Launch

When Apollo 13 launched into space on April 11, 1970, America was almost bored with space missions. Two other spacecrafts had already landed on the moon. Both had returned safely. No one was prepared for the drama about to unfold.

The Warnings

Training for the lunar mission was intense. Days before the Apollo 13 mission, the worst happened to the Command Module pilot. Ken Mattingly was pulled from the crew. He was exposed to the measles and had no immunity to the disease. Mattingly was replaced by a backup pilot.

Another bad sign was present. The No. 2 oxygen tank had trouble before the flight. In fact, it had been removed from Apollo 10. It failed tests before the launch of Apollo 13. Why didn't anyone fix it? NASA thought that it had.

The Accident

Fifty-six hours into the mission, the No. 2 oxygen tank exploded in the Service Module section. The explosion damaged the No. 1 oxygen tank, too. The supply of electricity, light, and water was soon lost. The three astronauts—James Lovell, John Swigert, and Fred Haise—knew they were in serious trouble!

The biggest goal was to get the crew back to Earth alive. Ground Control in Houston had to think of a way to bring them home safely. The astronauts could only use supplies that were onboard to solve the problem.

The Landing

Ground Control and the astronauts did some quick thinking. The crew moved from the damaged Command and Service Module into the Lunar Module. They used the Lunar Module as their "lifeboat." Using the sun as a guide, the crew burst back into Earth's atmosphere. The crew landed safely in the South Pacific. The mission was a "successful failure" because the astronauts survived.

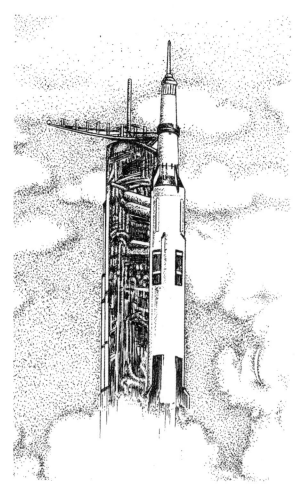

Apollo 13's mission was to land on the moon.

Nonfiction Reading Practice, Grade 6 • EMC 3317 • ©2003 by Evan-Moor Corp.

The Apollo 13 Mission

Fill in the bubble to answer each question or complete each sentence.

1. How many nautical miles from Earth was Apollo 13 when the explosion occurred?
   - Ⓐ   2,000
   - Ⓑ   20,000
   - Ⓒ   200,000
   - Ⓓ 2,000,000

2. Which of these is a synonym for the word *lunar*?
   - Ⓐ sun
   - Ⓑ star
   - Ⓒ spacecraft
   - Ⓓ moon

3. Which of these is true about the space crew of Apollo 13?
   - Ⓐ The original training crew went into space.
   - Ⓑ Three astronauts were part of the Apollo 13 crew.
   - Ⓒ Ken Mattingly became the new Command Module pilot on the mission.
   - Ⓓ The crew landed safely in the Atlantic Ocean.

4. Which gas leaked as a result of the explosion?
   - Ⓐ carbon dioxide
   - Ⓑ hydrogen
   - Ⓒ carbon monoxide
   - Ⓓ oxygen

5. The mission was labeled _____.
   - Ⓐ a successful failure
   - Ⓑ a disaster
   - Ⓒ a success
   - Ⓓ a failure

Bonus: On the back of this page, answer the following question: In what way was the mission a success?

Lunar Mission in Trouble

Peaceful Sign-off

On April 13, 1970, Ground Control workers had settled into a routine in Houston. Apollo 13 was 56 hours into its mission. Everything appeared to be going as planned. The crew had just said "good night" to America on a TV broadcast. Nine minutes later disaster struck!

The Shock

"Houston, we have a problem here." These chilling words put Americans at the edge of their seats. Apollo 13 was heading for disaster. Americans had already watched two lunar missions on TV go off without a hitch. No one could have known the terror that the three astronauts faced. They were floating in space with no way home.

The Problem

An explosion had destroyed the outside of the Command and Service Module named *Odyssey*. It had also blown up the No. 2 oxygen tank and damaged the No. 1 oxygen tank. Suddenly, the astronauts were in danger of losing heat, power, oxygen, and water. Astronaut James Lovell reported seeing some sort of gas leaking from the ship. It was oxygen, and it was leaking out fast.

The Fix

Ground Control faced their biggest challenge ever. They had to find a way to save the astronauts. Instead of taking months, or even years, to solve a problem, Ground Control had only minutes to save the astronauts. To save power, the astronauts turned off all controls that they didn't really need. With quick thinking and rationing of supplies and water, the crew managed to survive.

With 15 minutes of power left on the *Odyssey*, the crew made their way through a tunnel to the Lunar Module, *Aquarius*. *Aquarius* was their only way back to Earth.

The Lunar Module *Aquarius*

The Review

Four hours before landing, the crew shed the damaged *Odyssey*. Three hours later, the crew left *Aquarius* and splashed down into the Pacific Ocean.

Tests revealed that the No. 2 oxygen tank had been faulty. It had been removed from Apollo 10 for a related problem. Ground Control thought the problem was fixed. Fortunately, the astronauts survived the error. The mission became known as a "successful failure." Ground Control and the astronauts worked together to avoid complete disaster.

Name _____

Lunar Mission in Trouble

Fill in the bubble to answer each question or complete each sentence.

1. Ground Control for Apollo 13 was located _____.
   - Ⓐ on the moon
   - Ⓑ at Cape Canaveral, Florida
   - Ⓒ on TV
   - Ⓓ in Houston, Texas

2. How long had Apollo 13 been on its mission when the explosion occurred?
   - Ⓐ 2 days, 8 hours
   - Ⓑ 28 hours
   - Ⓒ 56 minutes
   - Ⓓ 5 days, 6 minutes

3. Which of these was <u>not</u> one of the strategies to save the crew?
   - Ⓐ rationed water
   - Ⓑ rationed supplies
   - Ⓒ studied the problem for a month
   - Ⓓ turned off unnecessary controls

4. The _____ was badly damaged on the lunar mission.
   - Ⓐ Apollo 13
   - Ⓑ Lunar Module
   - Ⓒ *Aquarius*
   - Ⓓ *Odyssey*

5. The faulty _____ was blamed as the cause of the explosion.
   - Ⓐ No. 1 oxygen tank
   - Ⓑ No. 2 oxygen tank
   - Ⓒ wiring on the control panel
   - Ⓓ heating system

Bonus: The three astronauts faced many terrifying moments on the Apollo 13 lunar mission. Pretend you were one of the astronauts. On the back of this page, write about the scariest moment for you on this mission to the moon.

The Successful Failure of a Mission

For the crew of Apollo 13, the dream of walking on the moon was close at hand. Command Module pilot, Ken Mattingly, was the first to have his dream shattered. Having been exposed to measles, Mattingly was disqualified from the flight. Apollo 13 took off on April 11, 1970. The launch went off without a hitch. The ship was headed for a region on the moon called Fra Mauro.

The Bust

Americans watched a live broadcast of the astronauts headed for the moon. This primitive version of "reality TV" showed the astronauts floating weightlessly. The mission was on track for success. Only 9 minutes after astronaut James Lovell said "good night" to America, the Command and Service Module, called *Odyssey,* began its nightmare.

A sharp bang and vibration jolted the *Odyssey.* An explosion destroyed oxygen tank No. 2, and the remaining tank was quickly leaking its contents into space. The astronauts were in serious danger. Ground Control determined that the *Odyssey* had 15 minutes of power left.

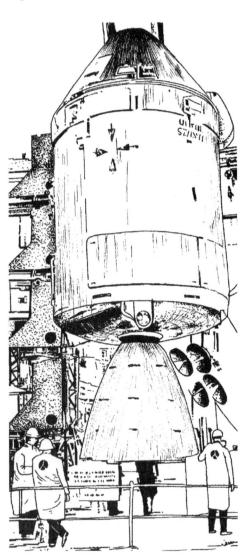

The crew was forced to seek refuge in the Lunar Module, *Aquarius.* The *Aquarius* was attached to the Command and Service Module. It was designed for the men to use in the landing on the moon, not to support three men on their return to Earth.

The Plan

The astronauts had to conserve power, heat, and water to survive in the *Aquarius.* Meanwhile, Ground Control devised a plan to keep the men from dying of dangerous carbon dioxide poisoning. Using plastic bags, cardboard, and tape—all supplies that the astronauts had onboard—they fixed the problem just in time. The three astronauts were on their way home.

After the Fact

In spite of careful planning and precautions, one big error was overlooked. The faulty oxygen tank No. 2 had a history of failure. Due to a number of contributing factors, including a change in permissible voltage to the heaters in the oxygen tanks, tank No. 2 was a bomb waiting to go off. The big error almost cost the astronauts their lives. The mission was declared a "successful failure" because the astronauts survived.

A whole panel of the Service Module section of *Odyssey* was blown off in the explosion.

Name _____

The Successful Failure of a Mission

Fill in the bubble to answer each question or complete each sentence.

1. Which of these is an antonym of the word *conserve*?
   - Ⓐ create
   - Ⓑ waste
   - Ⓒ save
   - Ⓓ produce

2. What happened to Command Module pilot Ken Mattingly?
   - Ⓐ He died in the explosion.
   - Ⓑ He became ill with the measles and was sent home.
   - Ⓒ He was disqualified from the flight due to measles exposure.
   - Ⓓ He saved the crew by using supplies onboard to fix the problem.

3. After the explosion, Ground Control determined that the *Odyssey* had _____ of power left.
   - Ⓐ 15 minutes
   - Ⓑ 56 minutes
   - Ⓒ 24 hours
   - Ⓓ 3 days

4. *Aquarius* is another name for _____.
   - Ⓐ the moon
   - Ⓑ the Command and Service Module
   - Ⓒ Ground Control
   - Ⓓ the Lunar Module

5. Which sentence is true about the Apollo 13 lunar mission?
   - Ⓐ An explosion on the *Odyssey* happened after the astronauts landed on the moon.
   - Ⓑ The faulty No. 1 oxygen tank caused the explosion.
   - Ⓒ The crew abandoned the *Odyssey* and boarded the *Aquarius*.
   - Ⓓ The astronauts suffered from carbon dioxide poisoning.

Bonus: On the back of this page, write what you think is meant by the title of this article "The Successful Failure of a Mission."

The International Space Station

Introducing the Topic

1. Reproduce page 71 for individual students, or make a transparency to use with a group or the whole class.

2. Show students the pictures of the International Space Station as it will look when completed in 2006. Share with students the interesting facts about the space station. Tell students that this is a collaborative effort involving 16 countries to build a permanent inhabited space station.

Reading the Selections

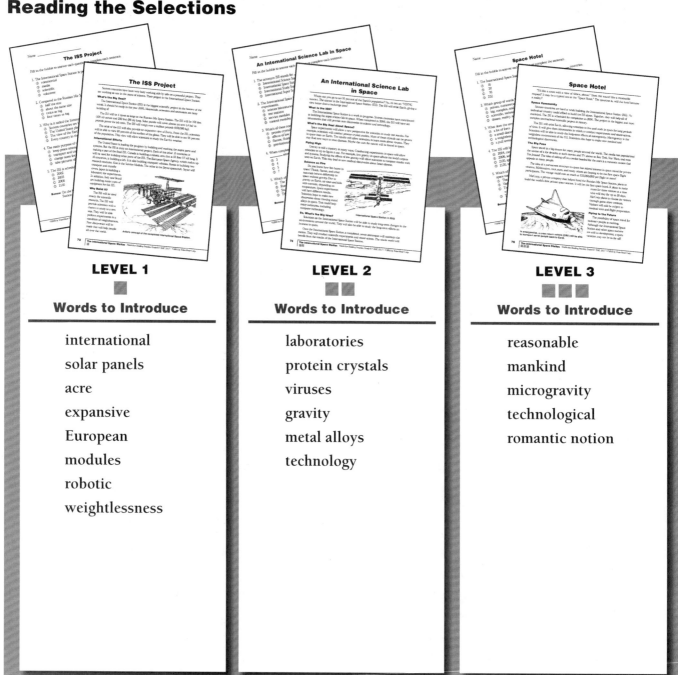

LEVEL 1

Words to Introduce

international

solar panels

acre

expansive

European

modules

robotic

weightlessness

LEVEL 2

Words to Introduce

laboratories

protein crystals

viruses

gravity

metal alloys

technology

LEVEL 3

Words to Introduce

reasonable

mankind

microgravity

technological

romantic notion

Nonfiction Reading Practice, Grade 6 • EMC 3317 • ©2003 by Evan-Moor Corp.

International Space Station

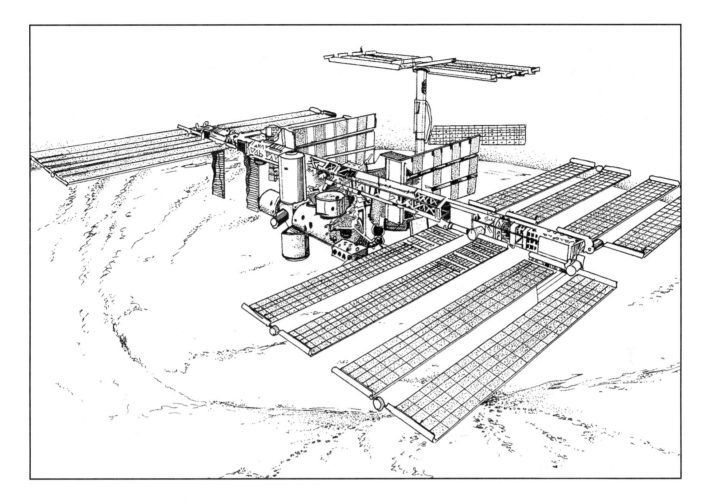

When completed, the International Space Station (ISS) will have the following major components:

- Control Module (command and control systems)

- Three Nodes (connect major portions of the ISS)

- Service Module (living quarters, docking ports, and rocket engines)

- Six Scientific Laboratories (contain scientific equipment and a robotic arm)

- Laboratory Module (environmental facility for research)

- Truss (tower-like spine for attaching modules and systems equipment)

- Mobile Servicing System (robotic system that will move along truss; equipped with remote arm for assembly and maintenance activities)

- Transfer Vehicles (*Soyuz* spacecraft for transport to and from Earth and crew-return vehicle called X-38 for emergency evacuation)

- Electrical Power System (solar panels and equipment for generating and storing power)

The ISS Project

Sixteen countries have been very busy working side by side on a peaceful project. They are working as one in the name of science. Their project is the International Space Station.

What's the Big Deal?

The International Space Station (ISS) is the biggest scientific project in the history of the world. It should be ready in the year 2006. Meanwhile, scientists and astronauts are busy building it!

The ISS will be 4 times as large as the Russian Mir Space Station. The ISS will be 356 feet (109 m) across and 290 feet (88 m) long. Solar panels will cover almost an acre (.4 ha) to provide power for lab tests. The ISS will weigh over a million pounds (450,000 kg).

The orbit of the ISS will also provide an expansive view of Earth. From the ISS, scientists will be able to view 85 percent of the surface of the globe. They will be able to see 95 percent of the population. This view will allow scientists to study the Earth's weather.

International Efforts

The United States is leading the program by building and working the major parts and systems. But the ISS is truly an international project. Each of the other 15 countries is making a part of the final ISS. Canada is building a robotic arm that is 55 feet (17 m) long. It will be used for building other parts of the ISS. The European Space Agency, which makes up 10 countries, is building a lab. It is also building transport vehicles. Russia is building two research modules. One is the Service Module. The other is the *Soyuz* spacecraft. *Soyuz* will transport and transfer crews. Japan is building a laboratory for experiments. In addition, Italy and Brazil are building many types of equipment for the ISS.

Why Build It?

The ISS will be used mostly for scientific research. The ISS will provide scientists with a chance to study in a new way. They will be able to perform experiments in a condition of weightlessness. New discoveries will be made that will help people all over the world.

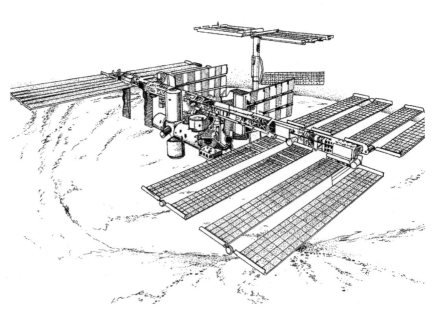

Artist's concept of the completed International Space Station.

Name _____

The ISS Project

Fill in the bubble to answer each question or complete each sentence.

1. The International Space Station is primarily a _____ project.
   - Ⓐ commercial
   - Ⓑ media
   - Ⓒ scientific
   - Ⓓ volunteer

2. Compared to the Russian Mir Space Station, it will be _____.
   - Ⓐ half the size
   - Ⓑ about the same size
   - Ⓒ twice as big
   - Ⓓ four times as big

3. Why is it called the International Space Station?
   - Ⓐ Sixteen countries are building it for all of mankind.
   - Ⓑ The United States plans to let other countries visit it.
   - Ⓒ The view of the Earth will be international.
   - Ⓓ Every country in the world has to pay for it.

4. The main purpose of the *Soyuz* is to _____.
   - Ⓐ keep peace among the nations
   - Ⓑ transport and transfer crews
   - Ⓒ charge taxes for use of the ISS
   - Ⓓ take pictures of Earth

5. The ISS is scheduled to be ready in the year _____.
   - Ⓐ 2002
   - Ⓑ 2003
   - Ⓒ 2006
   - Ⓓ 2110

Bonus: On the back of this page, explain the size of the International Space Station. Be sure to include facts and measurements.

An International Science Lab in Space

Where can you go to see 95 percent of the Earth's population? No, it's not an *NSYNC concert. The answer is the International Space Station (ISS). The ISS will orbit Earth, giving a view better than a backstage pass!

What Is the ISS?

The International Space Station is a work in progress. Sixteen countries have contributed to building the super science lab in space. When completed in 2006, the ISS will have six laboratories that will provide new discoveries in science and technology.

What's the Big Deal About Space?

Space experiments will allow a new perspective for scientists to study test results. For example, scientists will conduct protein crystal studies. More of these crystals can be grown in space than on Earth. The results will allow scientists to learn more about viruses. They may find new ways to treat diseases. Maybe the cure for cancer will be found in space.

Flying High

Gravity is still a mystery in many ways. Conducting experiments in space will allow scientists to try to figure it out. For example, low gravity in space affects the body's organs and systems. Studying the effects of low gravity will allow scientists to compare results with tests on Earth. This may lead to new medical discoveries about heart disease.

Science on Fire

Do you know how fire burns in space? Fluids, flames, and other materials behave differently in space without gravity. Due to gravity on Earth, air rises and falls with currents, depending on temperature. Space experiments will have different results. Scientists hope to make new discoveries about creating metal alloys in space. This could help many industries, including computer technology.

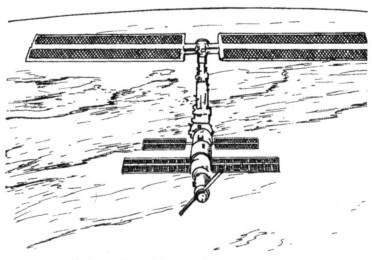

International Space Station in 2002

So, What's the Big Idea?

Scientists on the International Space Station will be able to study long-term changes in the environments around the world. They will also be able to study the long-term effects on humans in space.

Once the International Space Station is completed, seven astronauts will maintain the station. They will conduct scientific experiments and observations. The whole world will benefit from the results of the International Space Station.

Name _____

An International Science Lab in Space

Fill in the bubble to answer each question or complete each sentence.

1. The acronym *ISS* stands for _____.
   - Ⓐ International Science Station
   - Ⓑ International Space Station
   - Ⓒ International Study Station
   - Ⓓ International Super Science Lab

2. The International Space Station will have six _____ in which to conduct experiments.
   - Ⓐ science laboratories
   - Ⓑ test stations
   - Ⓒ service modules
   - Ⓓ control modules

3. Which of these research studies was <u>not</u> mentioned in the article?
   - Ⓐ protein crystal studies
   - Ⓑ effects of low gravity in space
   - Ⓒ flames, fluids, and metals in space
   - Ⓓ gravitational effects on plants

4. When completed, the International Space Station will be able to have _____ astronauts living and working in space.
   - Ⓐ 3
   - Ⓑ 4
   - Ⓒ 5
   - Ⓓ 7

5. Which of these statements shows a cooperative effort to build the ISS?
   - Ⓐ The ISS is being assembled piece by piece in space.
   - Ⓑ Russia made the first component of the ISS.
   - Ⓒ Sixteen countries are working together to build the ISS.
   - Ⓓ The ISS will be completed in the year 2006.

Bonus: On the back of this page, explain the advantages of conducting experiments in space.

Space Hotel

"I'd like a room with a view of Africa, please." Does this sound like a reasonable request? It may be a typical one at the "Space Hotel." The question is, will the hotel become a reality?

Space Community

Sixteen countries are hard at work building the International Space Station (ISS). No individual country could afford to build the ISS alone. Together, they will help all of mankind. The ISS is scheduled for completion in 2006. The project is the biggest and most complex international scientific project in history.

The ISS will orbit Earth, allowing scientists to live and work in space for long periods of time. It will give them laboratories in which to conduct experiments and observations. Scientists will be able to study the long-term effects of microgravity. Microgravity is the weightless environment of the ISS. Scientists also hope to make new medical and technological discoveries.

The Big Fuss

Space travel is a big dream for many people around the world. The media has popularized the notion of it for decades in such movies and TV shows as *Star Trek*, *Star Wars*, and even *The Jetsons*! The idea of taking off in a rocket headed for the stars is a romantic notion that appeals to many people.

The idea of a permanent structure in space has stirred interest in space travel for private citizens. Millionaires, rock stars, and many others are hoping to be the first space flight participants. The voyage could cost as much as $25,000,000 per flight or more!

MirCorp, a private company that helped fund the Russian Mir Space Station, plans to build the world's first private space station. It will be the first space hotel. It plans to make room for three visitors at a time who will stay for up to 20 days. MirCorp plans to choose its visitors through game show contests. Visitors will still be subject to medical tests and flight preparation.

In emergencies, a crew-return vehicle (CRV) will be able to transport seven people back to Earth.

Flying to the Future

The possibility of space travel for ordinary people is exciting. Although the International Space Station and other space stations are still in development, a space vacation may not be so far off!

Name _____

Use your own paper!

Space Hotel

Fill in the bubble to answer each question or complete the sentence.

1. The International Space Station is a collaborative effort of _____ countries.
   - Ⓐ   16
   - Ⓑ   20
   - Ⓒ   76
   - Ⓓ 232

2. Which group of words best describes the ISS project?
   - Ⓐ private, commercial, and hotel
   - Ⓑ big, complex, and expensive
   - Ⓒ scientific, technological, and international
   - Ⓓ dream, reality, and romantic notion

3. What does the term *microgravity* mean as used in this article?
   - Ⓐ a lot of force
   - Ⓑ a small discovery
   - Ⓒ a weightless environment
   - Ⓓ a pull toward Earth

4. The ISS will be completed in _____ and used for _____.
   - Ⓐ 2004, cancer research
   - Ⓑ 2006, scientific experiments and observations
   - Ⓒ 2110, space travel
   - Ⓓ 2120, technological discoveries

5. Which of these sentences is <u>not</u> true about plans to build a private space station?
   - Ⓐ The MirCorp Company is planning to build one.
   - Ⓑ Visitors could be chosen through game show contests.
   - Ⓒ The plan is to make room for three visitors at a time who will stay for up to 20 days.
   - Ⓓ The private space hotel is booked solid until 2012.

Bonus: On the back of this page, write a paragraph explaining the advantages or disadvantages of private companies expanding into space.

Rachel Carson

Introducing the Topic

1. Reproduce page 79 for individual students, or make a transparency to use with a group or the whole class.

2. Share with students the time line of Rachel Carson. Read and discuss the importance of this remarkable author, biologist, and environmentalist.

Reading the Selections

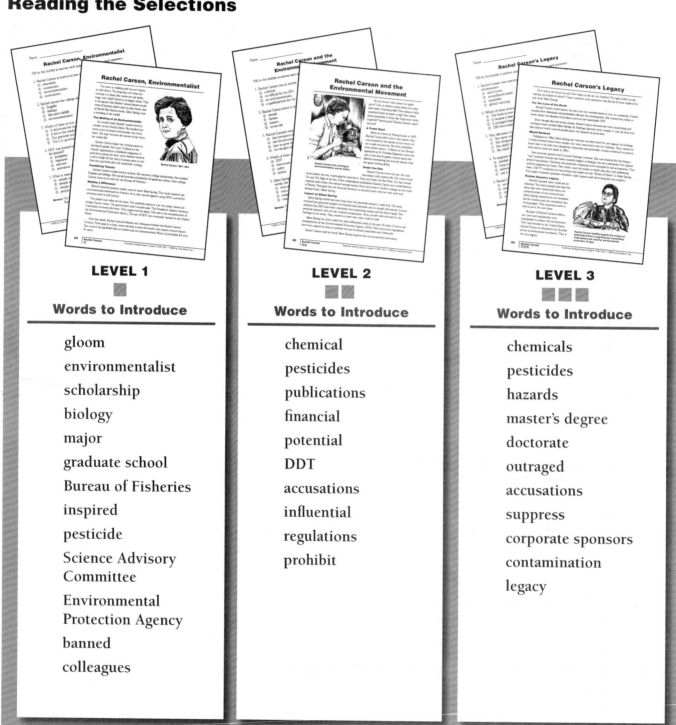

LEVEL 1

Words to Introduce

- gloom
- environmentalist
- scholarship
- biology
- major
- graduate school
- Bureau of Fisheries
- inspired
- pesticide
- Science Advisory Committee
- Environmental Protection Agency
- banned
- colleagues

LEVEL 2

Words to Introduce

- chemical
- pesticides
- publications
- financial
- potential
- DDT
- accusations
- influential
- regulations
- prohibit

LEVEL 3

Words to Introduce

- chemicals
- pesticides
- hazards
- master's degree
- doctorate
- outraged
- accusations
- suppress
- corporate sponsors
- contamination
- legacy

Time Line of Rachel Carson's Life

1907 — Born on May 27 in Springdale, Pennsylvania.

1917 — Stories published in children's magazine, *St. Nicholas*.

1029 — Graduated with honors from Pennsylvania College for Women.

1932 — Received master's degree in zoology from John Hopkins University.

1936 — Joined Bureau of Fisheries as a biologist.

1941 — Wrote *Under the Sea Wind*, a book about ocean life.

1951 — Wrote *The Sea Around Us*, a book about ocean life conservation.

1955 — Wrote *The Edge of the Sea*, an identification guide to ocean life.

1962 — Wrote *Silent Spring*, a book about chemical effects on the environment.

1963 — Named Conservationist of the Year by National Wildlife Federation.

1964 — Died on April 14 of cancer.

1980 — Carson's son accepted Presidential Medal of Freedom on her behalf.

Rachel Carson, Environmentalist

The snow is melting and the sun begins to beat down. The long days of winter are coming to a close. But where are the birds, bugs, and tulips? Earth is strangely silent. This is the gloom that Rachel Carson feared would come if humans didn't start to take better care of Earth! Her famous book, *Silent Spring,* sent a warning to the world.

Rachel Carson 1907–1964

The Making of an Environmentalist

As a small child, Rachel Carson loved to wander on her family's farm. She studied the many types of plants and animals that lived there. She kept this love for nature in her heart her whole life.

Rachel Carson began her writing career in the fourth grade. Her story "A Battle in the Clouds" appeared in a children's magazine. It paid her a penny for each word. Rachel received a silver badge for her story. It meant more to her than any paycheck she ever earned for writing.

Combining Talents

Rachel Carson studied hard in school. She earned a college scholarship. She studied English and biology. She earned another scholarship for graduate school. After college, Carson went on to work for the Bureau of Fisheries.

Making a Difference

Rachel Carson's greatest impact was her book *Silent Spring.* This book inspired the environmental movement in America. In it, she warned against using DDT, a powerful chemical used to kill insects.

The public took sides on the issue. The pesticide industry was very angry about the things Carson wrote. The government took Carson's side. The President's Science Advisory Committee reviewed the book. They supported her ideas. This led to the establishment of the Environmental Protection Agency. The use of DDT was eventually banned in the United States.

After her death, Rachel Carson's friends and colleagues formed the Rachel Carson Council. Their goal is to help others develop a sense of wonder and respect toward nature. The council has gathered data on health and the environmental effects of pesticides for over 35 years.

Nonfiction Reading Practice, Grade 6 • EMC 3317 • ©2003 by Evan-Moor Corp.

Name _____

Rachel Carson, Environmentalist

Fill in the bubble to answer each question or complete each sentence.

1. Rachel Carson is known as one of the first _____.
   - Ⓐ educators
   - Ⓑ economists
   - Ⓒ environmentalists
   - Ⓓ entertainers

2. Rachel earned her college degree in _____.
   - Ⓐ English
   - Ⓑ biology
   - Ⓒ fish and wildlife
   - Ⓓ environmentalism

3. Which of these is true of Rachel Carson's book *Silent Spring*?
   - Ⓐ It destroyed her reputation as a scientist.
   - Ⓑ It led to the establishment of the Environmental Protection Agency.
   - Ⓒ The pesticide industry approved of its findings.
   - Ⓓ The U.S. government opposed her views on environmental issues.

4. DDT was banned in the United States. Which of these words is a synonym for *banned*?
   - Ⓐ forbidden
   - Ⓑ legalized
   - Ⓒ allowed
   - Ⓓ permitted

5. What is meant by the term *environmental movement*?
   - Ⓐ people organizing protests
   - Ⓑ people writing books about nature
   - Ⓒ people moving around the country enjoying nature
   - Ⓓ people organizing to respect and protect nature

Bonus: On the back of this page, explain why *Silent Spring* was a good name for Rachel Carson's important book.

Rachel Carson and the Environmental Movement

Rachel Carson was a biologist, environmentalist, and an author.

Do you know what makes an apple grow? Sure, it needs a seed, some sun, rain, and water. Anything else? How about a little chemical boost to make it big? How about some pesticides to keep the bugs away while it grows? Sound good? Rachel Carson wasn't so sure!

A Fresh Start

Born on a farm in Pennsylvania in 1907, Rachel Carson fell in love with nature. She was amazed by the details of the beauty of the world around her. Her first published story about nature, "A Battle in the Clouds," appeared in *St. Nicholas Magazine* when she was in the fourth grade. Carson spent her lifetime combining her love for nature with her great writing skills.

Under the Sea

Rachel Carson loved the sea. She was fascinated with marine life. She wrote three books about the sea, expressing her love for it. They are *Under the Sea Wind*, *The Sea Around Us*, and *The Edge of the Sea*. These publications established Rachel Carson as a world-famous scientist and writer. She earned enough money from the books to build a cottage on the coast of Maine. This gave her the financial freedom to research and write her next and most famous book, *Silent Spring*.

Impact of *Silent Spring*

Silent Spring stirred up more bugs than the pesticide industry could kill. The book revealed the potential dangers of chemical and pesticide use for people and nature. Carson claimed that DDT and other chemicals were poisoning people and the food supply. The pesticide industry did not like Carson's accusations. Many people were alarmed by the findings in the book. They wanted to know how they could be safe.

Silent Spring has been called the most influential book of the past 50 years. It led to the establishment of the Environmental Protection Agency (EPA). Many laws and regulations have been passed to limit or prohibit the use of certain pesticides and chemicals.

Rachel Carson and her book *Silent Spring* inspired the environmental movement.

Nonfiction Reading Practice, Grade 6 • EMC 3317 • ©2003 by Evan-Moor Corp.

Name _____

Rachel Carson and the Environmental Movement

Fill in the bubble to answer each question or complete each sentence.

1. Rachel Carson was an author, a scientist, and _____.
   - Ⓐ a farmer
   - Ⓑ an official for the EPA
   - Ⓒ an environmentalist
   - Ⓓ a spokesperson for the pesticide industry

2. Rachel Carson loved to study and write about _____.
   - Ⓐ clouds
   - Ⓑ forests
   - Ⓒ insects
   - Ⓓ ocean life

3. Rachel Carson's most famous book, *Silent Spring*, is about _____.
   - Ⓐ the corruption in government
   - Ⓑ the Environmental Protection Agency
   - Ⓒ how to grow big crops with chemicals
   - Ⓓ the dangers of pesticide use on the environment

4. Which of these words does <u>not</u> belong with the word *pesticide*?
   - Ⓐ DDT
   - Ⓑ insecticide
   - Ⓒ safety
   - Ⓓ poison

5. *Silent Spring* is called the most influential book of the past 50 years. In other words, the book has _____.
   - Ⓐ been sold in a lot of bookstores
   - Ⓑ had a powerful effect on people's views about the environment
   - Ⓒ made people want to read more about nature
   - Ⓓ changed the way people think about the EPA

Bonus: On the back of this page, write a poem about Rachel Carson, highlighting her importance to the environmental movement.

Rachel Carson's Legacy

How safe is the food you eat? How clean is the air you breathe? Do high profits justify risking the health of others? These concerns were questions that Rachel Carson explored in her book *Silent Spring*.

For the Love of the Earth

Rachel Carson loved nature, but she was very worried about it, too. As a scientist, Carson studied how chemicals and pesticides affected the environment. She wanted the public to know about the dangers of products such as the insecticide DDT.

Even though she had breast cancer, Rachel Carson devoted her time researching and writing a book entitled *Silent Spring*. Its findings alarmed many people. It was the first time that anyone really warned people about the hazards of pesticides.

Mixed Reviews

Published in 1962, *Silent Spring* met extreme reactions both for and against its findings. Carson received letters from people who were concerned with her findings. They wanted to know how to be safe from dangerous chemicals and pesticides. Carson continued to answer their letters until her death in 1964.

Not everyone agreed with Carson's findings, however. She was attacked for not being a "real" scientist because she held a master's degree in biology, but not a doctorate (the highest level of education). Chemical and pesticide companies were outraged by her accusations. They tried to suppress her book. They didn't want the public to think that they were poisoning them. CBS TV scheduled an hour-long news report on the "Rivers of Death" in *Silent Spring*. Two major corporate sponsors withdrew their support and advertising for the program.

Rachel Carson's Legacy

Rachel Carson's voice could not be silenced. Too many people had read her ideas and were concerned about the contamination of our environment. *Silent Spring* remained on the bestseller list for months and was translated into 14 languages. This important book is still in print 40 years later.

Because of Rachel Carson's efforts, new laws and regulations were established to protect the environment. DDT was banned in the United States. Rachel Carson is considered the founder of the environmental movement. That is her true legacy.

Rachel Carson testified against the misuse of pesticides before congressional committees, emphasizing the need for environmental protection of laws.

Nonfiction Reading Practice, Grade 6 • EMC 3317 • ©2003 by Evan-Moor Corp.

Name _____

Rachel Carson's Legacy

Fill in the bubble to answer each question or complete each sentence.

1. Rachel Carson was concerned about the effects of _____ on the environment.
   - Ⓐ auto fumes
   - Ⓑ secondhand smoke
   - Ⓒ pesticides
   - Ⓓ global warming

2. Which of these sentences is <u>not</u> true about the book *Silent Spring*?
   - Ⓐ The book is now out of print and hard to find.
   - Ⓑ It became a best seller and was translated into 14 languages.
   - Ⓒ It outraged many chemical and pesticide companies.
   - Ⓓ CBS News featured part of her book on a report.

3. Why did some critics think Rachel wasn't a real scientist?
   - Ⓐ She never went to college.
   - Ⓑ She dropped out of high school.
   - Ⓒ She didn't have a master's degree.
   - Ⓓ She didn't have a doctorate.

4. To *suppress* the book *Silent Spring* means to _____.
   - Ⓐ publish it immediately
   - Ⓑ keep it from the public
   - Ⓒ advertise it on TV
   - Ⓓ sell it for a profit

5. Rachel Carson's work inspired the _____ movement.
   - Ⓐ environmental
   - Ⓑ pesticide
   - Ⓒ chemical
   - Ⓓ educational

Bonus: On the back of this page, write a tribute to Rachel Carson, highlighting why she is still considered an important figure in America.

Dangers of Smoking

Introducing the Topic

1. Reproduce page 87 for individual students, or make a transparency to use with a group or the whole class.

2. Share with students the shocking facts about cigarette smoking in the United States. Discuss with students why—after all the evidence and statistics that have been shown to them over and over again—some children and teens still start smoking.

Reading the Selections

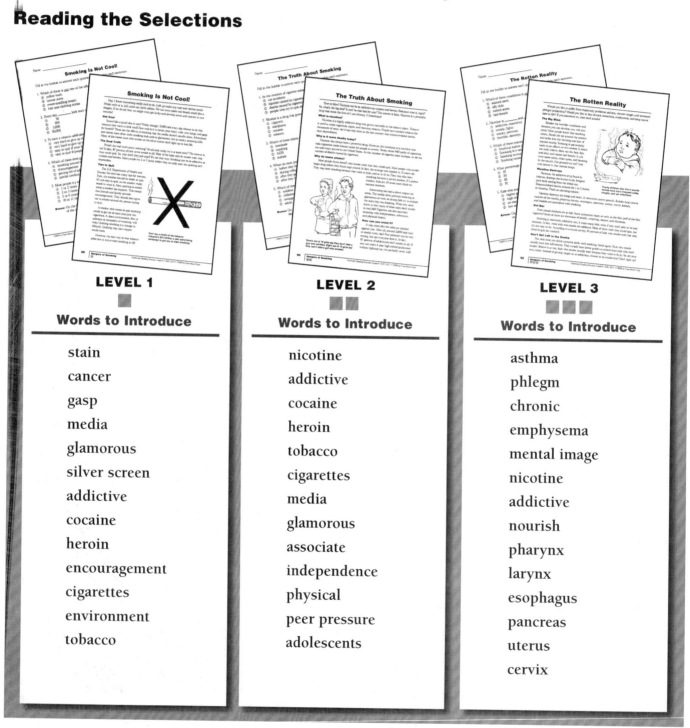

LEVEL 1
Words to Introduce

stain

cancer

gasp

media

glamorous

silver screen

addictive

cocaine

heroin

encouragement

cigarettes

environment

tobacco

LEVEL 2
Words to Introduce

nicotine

addictive

cocaine

heroin

tobacco

cigarettes

media

glamorous

associate

independence

physical

peer pressure

adolescents

LEVEL 3
Words to Introduce

asthma

phlegm

chronic

emphysema

mental image

nicotine

addictive

nourish

pharynx

larynx

esophagus

pancreas

uterus

cervix

Nonfiction Reading Practice, Grade 6 • EMC 3317 • ©2003 by Evan-Moor Corp.

The Shocking Facts and Figures About Smoking

- Ninety percent of all smokers started smoking before the age of 18.

- The average age of a new smoker is 13 years old.

- The concentration of carbon monoxide in tobacco is 800 times higher than the level considered safe by the U.S. Environmental Protection Agency.

- Cigarettes contain over 3,000 chemicals, and secondhand smoke contains about 4,000 chemicals.

- The chemicals in cigarettes include acetone (nail polish remover), hydrazine (rocket fuel), formaldehyde (preserving agent for dead animals), cyanide (rat poison), and ammonia (toilet bowl cleaner).

- Smoking affects the ability to think and move by reducing the oxygen supply to the brain.

- Smoking one cigarette can impair blood flow to the hand by 40 percent for up to an hour.

- Every 10 seconds somewhere in the world, someone dies from tobacco-related causes.

- Smoking causes more deaths than illegal drugs, homicides, car accidents, alcohol, and AIDS combined.

- Secondhand smoke kills 50,000 Americans each year, making it the leading cause of preventable death.

Smoking Is Not Cool!

Hey, I know something really cool to do. Let's go make our hair and clothes smell. While we're at it, let's stain our teeth yellow. We can even make our breath smell like a dragon. If we do all this, we might even get lucky and develop sores and cancers in our mouths!

Not Cool

Sound like a good idea to you? Oddly enough, 3,000 kids every day choose to do this because they want to look cool! How cool is it to strain your heart, ruin your lungs, and gasp for breath? These are the effects of smoking that the media doesn't usually show. Advertisers and movie stars often make smoking look cool or glamorous, but in reality, smoking kills. Many of the movie stars who smoke on the silver screen don't light up in real life.

The Real Truth

What's the real truth about smoking? Do all kids really try it at least once? The answer is no! In fact, 87 percent of kids never smoke at all. Most of the kids who do smoke wish that they could quit. So, why don't they just stop? It's not that easy. Smoking can be as addictive as cocaine and heroin. Most people try 2 or 3 times before they actually quit, but quitting isn't impossible.

Tips to Quit

The U.S. Department of Health and Human Services has many tips for success. First, the smoker should be ready to quit. It's not easy to quit, so the smoker really needs to want it. Also, quitting is easiest when a smoker has support. This means that friends and family provide encouragement. They should also agree not to smoke around the person trying to quit.

A smoker who wants to quit smoking needs to get rid of more than just the cigarettes. A clean environment, free of ashtrays or reminders of smoking, will help. Quitting smoking is a change in lifestyle. Quitting may also require medication.

Don't be a victim of the tobacco industry's $6.2 billion a year advertising campaign to get you to start smoking!

However, the best way to beat tobacco addiction is not to start smoking at all!

Name _____

Smoking Is Not Cool!

Fill in the bubble to answer each question or complete each sentence.

1. Which of these is <u>not</u> one of the effects of smoking?
   - Ⓐ yellow teeth
   - Ⓑ cancer sores
   - Ⓒ sweet-smelling breath
   - Ⓓ hair and clothing stinks

2. Every day, _____ kids start to smoke.
   - Ⓐ 30
   - Ⓑ 300
   - Ⓒ 3,000
   - Ⓓ 30,000

3. To have a tobacco *addiction* means it is _____.
   - Ⓐ very hard to give up the habit of smoking
   - Ⓑ very hard to give up smoking when you are young
   - Ⓒ easy to quit if your family and friends support you
   - Ⓓ easy to quit if people change their lifestyle

4. Which of these does <u>not</u> help a smoker to quit smoking?
   - Ⓐ smoking around him or her
   - Ⓑ encouragement
   - Ⓒ getting rid of ashtrays and cigarettes
   - Ⓓ special medication

5. Most people try to quit smoking _____ before they are successful.
   - Ⓐ 1 or 2 times
   - Ⓑ 2 or 3 times
   - Ⓒ 5 or 6 times
   - Ⓓ 10 or 11 times

Bonus: On the back of this page, write four things a smoker could do to get rid of the nasty habit.

The Truth About Smoking

True or false? Nicotine can be as addictive as cocaine and heroin. Everyone tries it, right? So, what's the big deal? It can't be that bad for you! The answer is false. Nicotine is a powerful drug that steals the lives of 1 out of every 5 Americans!

What is nicotine?

Nicotine is a highly addictive drug that grows naturally in the tobacco plant. Tobacco is used to make cigarettes, cigars, and chewing tobacco. People have smoked tobacco for thousands of years, but it has only been in the last century that tobacco-related deaths have skyrocketed.

Why is it more deadly today?

Nicotine has always been a powerful drug. However, the invention of a machine that rolls cigarettes made tobacco easier for people to smoke. Today, about 840 packs of cigarettes are sold every second in the United States. As the number of cigarette sales increase, so do the number of deaths caused by cigarettes.

Why do teens smoke?

Most people (even teens!) who smoke wish that they could quit. Most people who smoke begin long before they finish high school. In fact, the average new smoker is 13 years old. They may start smoking because they want to look cool or to fit in. They may also start smoking because a parent smokes. If a parent smokes, kids are 10 times more likely to become smokers.

Advertising has had a direct impact on teens. The media often portrays smoking as glamorous or cool, so young kids try to imitate the stars they see smoking. What they don't know is that many of those stars don't smoke in real life! Cigarette ads also associate smoking with independence, adventure, and physical beauty.

How can you avoid it?

It may seem like the odds are stacked against you. After all, around 3,000 kids start to smoke every day! Peer pressure can be very strong, but not everyone does it. In fact, 87 percent of adolescents don't smoke at all. If you can make it past high school graduation without lighting up, you probably never will!

Seven out of 10 girls say they won't date a guy who smokes. Eight out of 10 guys say they won't date a girl who smokes.

Name _____

The Truth About Smoking

Fill in the bubble to answer each question or complete each sentence.

1. As the number of cigarette sales increase, so do the number of _____.
   - Ⓐ car accidents
   - Ⓑ injuries caused by cigarettes
   - Ⓒ deaths caused by cigarettes
   - Ⓓ people who try to quit smoking

2. *Nicotine* is a drug that grows in the _____ plant.
   - Ⓐ cigarette
   - Ⓑ marijuana
   - Ⓒ cocaine
   - Ⓓ tobacco

3. Which of these claims more lives in the U.S.?
   - Ⓐ homicide
   - Ⓑ smoking
   - Ⓒ AIDS
   - Ⓓ suicide

4. When do most people start smoking?
   - Ⓐ before they finish high school
   - Ⓑ during college
   - Ⓒ after they get married
   - Ⓓ after they have children

5. Which of these is a synonym for the word *adolescents*?
   - Ⓐ toddlers
   - Ⓑ children
   - Ⓒ teenagers
   - Ⓓ adults

Bonus: On the back of this page, design an ad to warn adolescents about the dangers of smoking.

The Rotten Reality

Would you like to suffer from respiratory problems, asthma, chronic cough, and increased phlegm production? Would you like to face chronic bronchitis, emphysema, and lung cancer later in life? If you answered no, then don't smoke!

The Big Stink

Besides the horrible conditions and diseases you can develop, you will also stink! Most people know that smoking stinks, floods the air around the smoker, and sinks into the clothing and hair of anyone nearby. Smoking is particularly nasty in its effects on the smoker. It stains the teeth yellow; dries out the hair, lips, and skin; and causes bad breath. It can even cause sores, white spots, and bleeding in the mouth. Not grossed out yet? Add oral cancer to that mental image.

Nicotine Destroys

Nicotine, the addictive drug found in tobacco, destroys the human body. Imagine your body rotting from the inside out. Tobacco-related deaths account for 1 in 5 deaths in America. That's an alarming statistic.

Young children who live in smoky homes have more frequent colds, coughs, and ear infections.

Nicotine destroys the lungs and heart. It nourishes cancer growth. Besides lung cancer, cancers of the mouth, pharynx, larynx, esophagus, pancreas, uterus, cervix, kidney, and bladder are associated with smoking.

Not Me!

Even casual smokers are at risk. Some symptoms begin as early as the first puff of the first cigarette! Some of these are shortness of breath, coughing, nausea, and dizziness.

Smoking is extremely addictive, too. It traps many kids, even if they don't plan to be real smokers. In fact, most kids who smoke are addicted. Most of them wish they could quit, but it's not easy to do. According to a recent survey, 40 percent of kids who smoke said that they tried to quit but couldn't.

Don't Get Left in the Smoke

The next time you think someone looks cool smoking, think again. Kids who smoke usually have low self-esteem. They usually have lower grades in school than kids who don't smoke. Believe it or not, kids who smoke usually start because they want to fit in. So, set your own trend. Instead of getting caught in an addiction, choose to be smoke-free! Don't light up!

Name _____

The Rotten Reality

Fill in the bubble to answer each question or complete each sentence.

1. Which of these conditions is <u>not</u> an effect of smoking?
   - Ⓐ stained teeth
   - Ⓑ oily skin
   - Ⓒ mouth sores
   - Ⓓ bad breath

2. Nicotine is _____ and _____ cancer growth.
   - Ⓐ addictive, nourishes
   - Ⓑ trendy, fights
   - Ⓒ smoky, prevents
   - Ⓓ horrible, destroys

3. Which of these statements is a statistic about smoking?
   - Ⓐ Smoking makes people look cool.
   - Ⓑ Smoking is a nasty habit.
   - Ⓒ Smoking accounts for 1 in 5 deaths in America.
   - Ⓓ Smoking causes many cancers.

4. What percentage of kids who smoke say they tried to quit but couldn't?
   - Ⓐ 10
   - Ⓑ 20
   - Ⓒ 40
   - Ⓓ 70

5. Kids who smoke usually have _____.
   - Ⓐ higher grades in school
   - Ⓑ high self-esteem
   - Ⓒ an easy time quitting
   - Ⓓ low self-esteem

Bonus: On the back of this page, explain why you think some adolescents still smoke, even though they know the rotten reality of it all.

Internet Safety

Introducing the Topic

1. Reproduce page 95 for individual students, or make a transparency to use with a group or the whole class.

2. Ask students how many of them use the Internet at home. Share with students that there is a need to be safe when surfing on the World Wide Web. Read and discuss the safety rules for using the Internet.

Reading the Selections

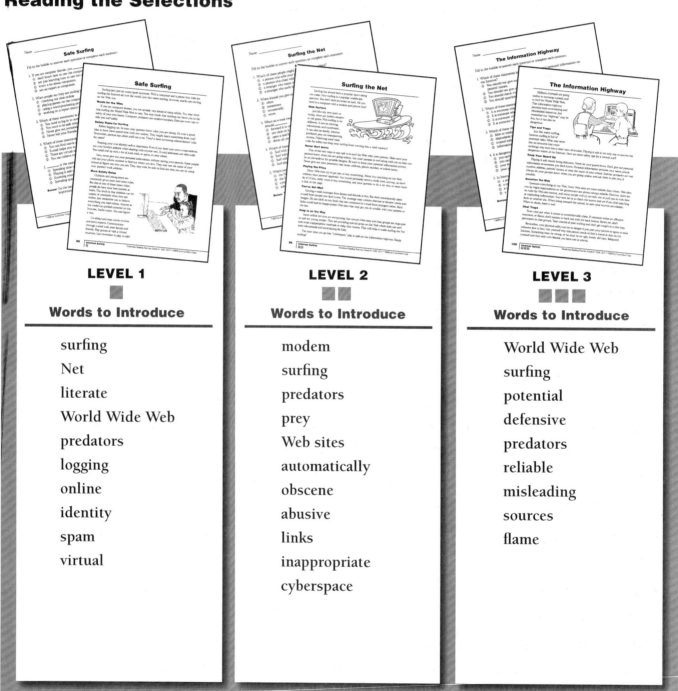

LEVEL 1	LEVEL 2	LEVEL 3
Words to Introduce	**Words to Introduce**	**Words to Introduce**
surfing	modem	World Wide Web
Net	surfing	surfing
literate	predators	potential
World Wide Web	prey	defensive
predators	Web sites	predators
logging	automatically	reliable
online	obscene	misleading
identity	abusive	sources
spam	links	flame
virtual	inappropriate	
	cyberspace	

Nonfiction Reading Practice, Grade 6 • EMC 3317 • ©2003 by Evan-Moor Corp.

Internet Safety Rules

- Do not give out personal information, such as address, telephone number, or parents' work address and telephone number without your parents' permission. (This gives strangers easy access to you.)

- Do not give out the name and location of your school without your parents' and school's permission. (That information can be sent instantaneously to hundreds of people.)

- Do not click on any links that are contained in e-mail from persons you do not know. (The links may be illegal or inappropriate sites that will get you in trouble with your parents and maybe the law.)

- Do not "chat" with strangers online. (That 12-year-old girl may really be a dangerous 40-year-old man!)

- Do not send pictures of yourself to strangers online. (Pictures can also be transmitted fast to strangers who try to exploit children.)

- Do not believe everything you read online. Remember, it may not be true. (Any offer that's "too good to be true" probably is.)

- If you stumble upon inappropriate sites on a search engine, tell your parents right away. (Your parents should have filtering features built in to your Internet browser that limit access to inappropriate sites for you.)

Safe Surfing

Surfing isn't just an ocean sport anymore. With a computer and a phone line, kids are surfing the Internet all over the world. Just like water surfing, however, sharks are circling on the Web, too.

Words for the Wise

If you are computer literate, you are already way ahead of many adults. You may think that surfing the World Wide Web is easy. You may think that nothing can harm you in the safety of your own home. Computer predators are modern burglars. Here are some tips to help you surf safely.

Safety Rules for Surfing

Before logging on, be sure your parents know what you are doing. It's even a good idea to have them spend time with you online. They might learn something from you! Remember, parents can often sniff out a rat. They've been screening telemarketers' calls for years!

Keeping your true identity safe is important. Even if you have your own e-mail address, use your family's address when dealing with anyone new. E-mail addresses are often sold. You could end up with a lot of junk mail, or spam, in your inbox.

Also, never give out your personal information without asking your parents. Some people will use your phone number to find out where you live. They may use the name of your school to figure out who you are. They may even be able to find out who you are by using your parents' work address.

More Safety Rules

Children and young teens are constantly given more and more rules. But this is one of those times when people do have your best interest at heart. The truth is that children can be targets of criminals when they are online. Just remember not to believe everything you read online. Anyone in the world can publish material on the Internet. You're smart. You can figure it out.

Go ahead and read movie reviews and news reports. Communicate through e-mail with your family and friends. Play games or visit a virtual museum. Just remember to play it safe!

Name _____

Safe Surfing

Fill in the bubble to answer each question or complete each sentence.

1. If you are *computer literate*, you _____.
   - Ⓐ don't know how to use the computer very well
   - Ⓑ are just learning how to use the computer
   - Ⓒ know a lot about computers
   - Ⓓ are an expert at computers

2. When people say they are *surfing the Net*, they are _____.
   - Ⓐ checking out sites online
   - Ⓑ playing games on the computer
   - Ⓒ using a word-processing program
   - Ⓓ working on a report about surfing

3. Which of these statements is an Internet safety rule?
   - Ⓐ You need to log in to access the World Wide Web.
   - Ⓑ You need to be safe when you are on the Internet.
   - Ⓒ Never give out personal information on the Internet.
   - Ⓓ Never tell your friends what you are researching on the Internet.

4. Which of these statements is <u>not</u> true about the Internet?
   - Ⓐ You can find movie reviews on the Internet.
   - Ⓑ E-mail helps you to stay in touch with family and friends.
   - Ⓒ There are virtual museums to visit on the Internet.
   - Ⓓ You can believe everything you read on the Internet.

5. _____ is the most important rule to follow when you're on the Internet.
   - Ⓐ Spending time on the Internet
   - Ⓑ Playing it safe on the Internet
   - Ⓒ Knowing your e-mail address
   - Ⓓ Spending quality time on the Internet

Bonus: On the back of this page, choose which safety rule you think is the most important one to remember and why.

Surfing the Net

Surfing has always been a popular sport along the coast. Now surfing is a popular worldwide pastime. You don't need an ocean to surf. All you need is a computer with a modem and phone line!

Risk Factors

Just like any new sport or hobby, there are hidden dangers in the game. Web surfing is no different. It can be exciting, educational, and convenient. It can also be deadly. Internet predators prey on unsuspecting victims. Following some basic rules for safety can keep your surfing from turning into a total wipeout!

Never Surf Alone

One of the best ways to stay safe is to surf the Web with your parents. Make sure your parents know when you are going online. Ask your parents to surf along with you so they can be on the lookout for possible dangers. Be sure to keep your personal information private. Never give out your password, real name, address, phone number, or school name.

Paying the Price

Many Web sites try to get you to buy something. Never buy anything on the Web without your parents' approval. You would probably need a credit card, anyway, so don't do it! If you really want to buy something, ask your parents to do it for you, or send them a link to the page.

You've Got Mail

Getting e-mail messages from family and friends is fun. But don't automatically open e-mail from people you don't know. The message may contain obscene or abusive words and images. Do not click on any links that are contained in e-mail from strangers either. Such links could lead to inappropriate Web sites that may get you in trouble with your parents or the law.

Help Is on the Way

Some online services are recognizing that certain Web sites and chat groups are improper or safe for young people. They are providing special areas on the Web where kids can surf and avoid inappropriate materials or risky chat rooms. This will help to make surfing the Net both educational and entertaining for kids.

The next time you go into "cyberspace," play it safe on the information highway. Happy surfing!

Name _____

Surfing the Net

Fill in the bubble to answer each question or complete each statement.

1. Which of these people might be an Internet predator?
   - Ⓐ a person who sells your parents something
   - Ⓑ a person who chats with his friends online
   - Ⓒ a stranger who wants to meet you in person
   - Ⓓ a stranger who surfs the Net

2. When should you give out your password to someone online?
   - Ⓐ often
   - Ⓑ sometimes
   - Ⓒ occasionally
   - Ⓓ never

3. When an e-mail message from a stranger has an attachment or link, you should _____.
   - Ⓐ forward it to your parents so they can report it to the police
   - Ⓑ not click on it because it may contain inappropriate words and images
   - Ⓒ open it and forward it to friends
   - Ⓓ delete all your e-mail messages

4. Which of these is one of the best ways to stay safe when surfing the Web?
   - Ⓐ Surf with your parents or let them know you are online.
   - Ⓑ Surf with your little brother or sister and show them how to get online.
   - Ⓒ Surf with your friends and go into group chat rooms together.
   - Ⓓ Surf alone and find interesting, offbeat Web sites.

5. Which term was not used to describe the World Wide Web in this article?
   - Ⓐ the Net
   - Ⓑ the Surfer
   - Ⓒ cyberspace
   - Ⓓ information highway

Bonus: This article told you what not to do on the Internet. On the back of this page, write four things you could do on the Internet that would be educational or just safe fun.

The Information Highway

Millions of people are going online to exchange e-mails and to surf the World Wide Web. This information highway provides both entertaining and educational resources. Just remember the "highway" may be fun, but it can also be dangerous.

Tips and Traps

Just like water surfing, Internet surfing is full of potential risks. What may seem like an innocent chat room exchange may turn into a tidal wave of trouble. Playing it safe is the only way to survive the dangerous waters of the Internet. Here are some safety tips for a smooth surf!

Keep Your Guard Up

Playing it safe means being defensive. Never let your guard down. Don't give out personal information to someone you don't know. Personal information includes your name, phone number, address, parents' names, or even the name of your school. Internet predators are real. Always let your parents know when you are going online, and ask them to join you, if possible.

Question the Web

Question everything on the Web. Some Web sites are more reliable than others. Web sites run by major organizations or the government are almost always reliable. However, there are no rules for Web site content, and many people will try to trick you or pull you in with false or misleading information. Your best bet is to check the source and see if you find matching facts on another site. When doing research for school, be sure your sources are reliable. When in doubt, leave it out!

Chat Traps

Trust your gut when it comes to uncomfortable chats. If someone writes an offensive comment, or flame, don't hesitate to back out with the back button. Better yet, don't participate in chat groups. Take control of your surfing and don't get caught in a chat trap.

Remember, your physical safety can be in danger if you post your picture or agree to meet someone face to face. Ask yourself why this person needs to find a friend or date on the Internet. Something must be wrong, or he must be an ugly, lonely old man. Safeguard yourself and chat only with friends you have met at school.

Name _____

The Information Highway

Fill in the bubble to answer each question or complete each sentence.

1. Which of these statements is true about giving out personal information on the Internet?
   Ⓐ You should not give out your name, but it's safe to give your parents' names.
   Ⓑ You should not give out your name, phone number, or address.
   Ⓒ You should check with your school before you use its name online.
   Ⓓ You should question everything on the Web.

2. Which of these statements describes an Internet predator?
   Ⓐ It is someone who hunts for information online.
   Ⓑ It is someone who likes to give false and misleading information.
   Ⓒ It is someone who preys on children for his or her own pleasure.
   Ⓓ It is someone who likes to talk in chat rooms.

3. Which of these means the opposite of *reliable information*?
   Ⓐ false or misleading information
   Ⓑ dependable information
   Ⓒ trusted information
   Ⓓ information given out by government offices

4. It is dangerous to visit a chat room online because _____.
   Ⓐ you can't be sure the people will keep a secret
   Ⓑ you can't be sure you are talking with people who are safe
   Ⓒ your feelings may be hurt by some of the comments made
   Ⓓ your parents will be angry with you

5. In Internet terms, an *offensive comment* is called _____.
   Ⓐ a predator
   Ⓑ a trick
   Ⓒ a chat
   Ⓓ a flame

Bonus: On the back of this page, design a brochure that would appeal to teens about Internet safety. Be sure to include at least three safety rules in your brochure.

Joseph Pilates

Introducing the Topic

1. Reproduce page 103 for individual students, or make a transparency to use with a group or the whole class.

2. Ask students what kinds of exercises they do to stay fit. Then show students the chart of pictures of the Pilates exercises. Share with students that these exercises have been around for almost 100 years. Joseph Pilates devised exercises and equipment that is one of the newest fitness trends today.

Reading the Selections

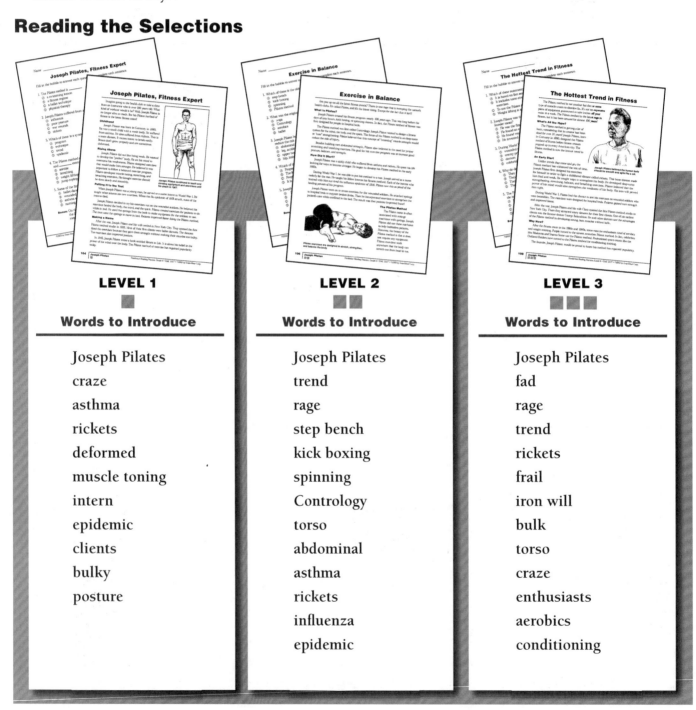

LEVEL 1

Words to Introduce

Joseph Pilates

craze

asthma

rickets

deformed

muscle toning

intern

epidemic

clients

bulky

posture

LEVEL 2

Words to Introduce

Joseph Pilates

trend

rage

step bench

kick boxing

spinning

Contrology

torso

abdominal

asthma

rickets

influenza

epidemic

LEVEL 3

Words to Introduce

Joseph Pilates

fad

rage

trend

rickets

frail

iron will

bulk

torso

craze

enthusiasts

aerobics

conditioning

Pilates Exercises and Equipment

Joseph Pilates devised exercises in the early 1900s that are still used today.

The most popular and versatile piece of Pilates' equipment was the reformer. This is a modern version of one.

Joseph Pilates, Fitness Expert

Imagine going to the health club to take a class from an instructor who is over 100 years old. What kind of workout would it be? Well, Joseph Pilates is no longer alive to teach. But his Pilates method of fitness is the latest fitness craze!

Childhood

Joseph Pilates was born in Germany in 1880. He was a small child with a weak body. He suffered from asthma. He also suffered from rickets. This is a bone disease. It causes bones to break easily. Bones don't grow properly and are sometimes deformed.

Rising Above

Joseph Pilates did not like being weak. He wanted to develop the "perfect" body. He set his mind to overcome his weaknesses. Pilates designed exercises that would make him stronger. He believed it was important to follow a balanced exercise program. Pilates developed muscle toning, stretching, and breathing exercises. He thought exercise should be done slowly and smoothly.

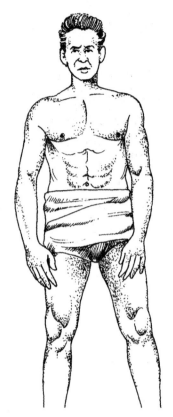

Joseph Pilates continued to teach and develop equipment and exercises until his death in 1967.

Putting It to the Test

When Joseph Pilates was a young man, he served as a nurse intern in World War I. He taught other interns his new exercises. When the flu epidemic of 1918 struck, none of the interns died.

Joseph Pilates decided to try his exercises out on the wounded soldiers. He believed his exercises healed the body, the mind, and the spirit. Pilates created exercises for patients to do while in bed. He used the springs from the beds to make equipment for the soldiers to use. The men used the springs to move in bed. Patients improved faster doing the Pilates method.

Making a Name

After the war, Joseph Pilates and his wife settled in New York City. They opened the first Pilates method studio in 1926. Most of their first clients were ballet dancers. The dancers liked the exercises because they gave them strength without making their muscles too bulky. The exercises also improved posture.

In 1945, Joseph Pilates wrote a book entitled *Return to Life*. It is about his belief in the power of the mind over the body. The Pilates method of exercise has regained popularity today.

Name _____

Joseph Pilates, Fitness Expert

Fill in the bubble to answer each question or complete each sentence.

1. The *Pilates method* is _____.
   - Ⓐ a swimming lesson
   - Ⓑ a fitness regime
   - Ⓒ a ballet technique
   - Ⓓ physical therapy

2. Joseph Pilates suffered from asthma and _____ as a child.
   - Ⓐ influenza
   - Ⓑ poor posture
   - Ⓒ war wounds
   - Ⓓ rickets

3. Which of these is a synonym for the word *craze*?
   - Ⓐ program
   - Ⓑ technique
   - Ⓒ trend
   - Ⓓ epidemic

4. The Pilates method combines muscle toning, stretching, and _____ exercises.
   - Ⓐ aerobic
   - Ⓑ breathing
   - Ⓒ weight lifting
   - Ⓓ jump roping

5. Some of the first clients of the Pilates studio were _____.
   - Ⓐ ballet dancers
   - Ⓑ wounded soldiers
   - Ⓒ asthma sufferers
   - Ⓓ nursing interns

Bonus: On the back of this page, write at least three things you learned about the Pilates method. Then answer this question: Do you think the Pilates method is a good exercise program? Why or why not?

Exercise in Balance

Are you up on all the latest fitness trends? There is one rage that is sweeping the nation's health clubs. It's called Pilates, and it's the latest thing. Except for the fact that it isn't!

What Is Pilates?

Joseph Pilates created his fitness program nearly 100 years ago. This was long before the days of step bench, kick boxing, or spinning classes. In fact, the Pilates method of fitness was first designed for people in hospital beds.

The Pilates method was first called Contrology. Joseph Pilates wanted to design a fitness system for the mind, the body, and the spirit. The focus of the Pilates method is on deep-torso or "core" strengthening. Pilates believed that this concept of "centering" muscle strength would reduce the risk of injury.

Besides building core abdominal strength, Pilates also believed in the need for proper stretching and breathing exercises. His goal for his exercise program was to increase good posture, balance, and strength.

How Did It Start?

Joseph Pilates was a sickly child who suffered from asthma and rickets. He spent his life looking for ways to become stronger. He began to develop his Pilates method in the early 1900s.

During World War I, he was able to put his method to a test. Joseph served as a nurse orderly for the war. He taught his fellow interns his fitness method. Each of the interns who trained with him survived the influenza epidemic of 1918. Pilates saw this as proof of the healing powers of his program.

Joseph Pilates went on to create exercises for the wounded soldiers. He attached springs to hospital beds to support broken limbs. Then he incorporated exercises to strengthen the patient's core while confined to the bed. The result was that patients improved faster!

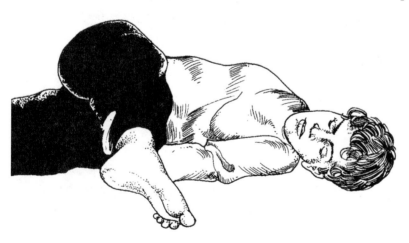

Pilates exercises are designed to stretch, strengthen, and balance the body.

The Pilates Method

The Pilates name is often associated with strange machines with springs. Joseph Pilates did use these machines to help bedridden patients. However, the beauty of the Pilates method is that it does not require any equipment. Pilates exercises work anywhere that the body can stretch out from head to toe.

Nonfiction Reading Practice, Grade 6 • EMC 3317 • ©2003 by Evan-Moor Corp.

Name _____

Exercise in Balance

Fill in the bubble to answer each question or complete each sentence.

1. Which of these is the oldest method of exercise?
   Ⓐ step bench
   Ⓑ kick boxing
   Ⓒ spinning
   Ⓓ Pilates method

2. What was the original name for the Pilates method?
   Ⓐ yoga
   Ⓑ Contrology
   Ⓒ aerobics
   Ⓓ ballet

3. Joseph Pilates believed it was important to build strong _____ muscles to reduce the risk of _____.
   Ⓐ abdominal, injury
   Ⓑ leg, accidents
   Ⓒ upper body, heart disease
   Ⓓ hip, imbalance

4. Which of these statements is not true about the Pilates method?
   Ⓐ Proper stretching and breathing exercises are important.
   Ⓑ The focus is on deep-torso strengthening.
   Ⓒ People need to use Pilates equipment to reach their goal for fitness.
   Ⓓ It is a fitness program that focuses on the mind, body, and spirit.

5. Joseph Pilates created his method nearly _____ years ago.
   Ⓐ 50
   Ⓑ 75
   Ⓒ 80
   Ⓓ 100

Bonus: On the back of this page, explain how the Pilates name came to be associated with strange machines with springs.

The Hottest Trend in Fitness

The Pilates method is not another fad diet or some type of miracle cream to dissolve fat. It's not an expensive piece of equipment guaranteed to take inches off your waist in a week. The Pilates method is the latest rage in fitness, but it has been around for almost 100 years!

What's All the Hype?

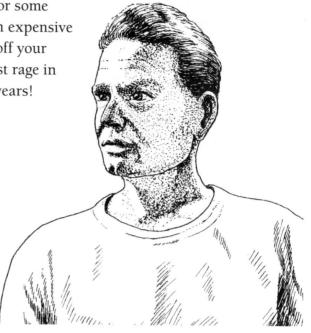

Joseph Pilates believed the human body should be smooth and agile like a cat.

The Pilates method is getting a lot of buzz, considering that its creator has been dead for over 35 years! Joseph Pilates, born in Germany in 1880, designed the Pilates method of fitness before fitness centers popped up in every American city. The Pilates method is now the hottest trend in fitness.

An Early Start

Unlike trends that come and go, the Pilates method has withstood the test of time. Joseph Pilates first designed his exercises for himself in order to fight a childhood disease called rickets. This bone disease made him frail and weak. He sought ways to strengthen his body. He developed deep-torso strengthening, stretching, balance, and breathing exercises. Pilates believed that the power of his mind would also strengthen the weakness of his body. His iron will proved him right.

During World War I, Pilates had the chance to test his exercises on wounded soldiers who were bedridden. The exercises were designed for hospital beds. Patients gained core strength and improved faster.

After the war, Joseph Pilates and his wife Clara opened the first Pilates method studio in New York City. There they attracted many dancers for their first clients. One of his earliest clients was the famous dancer George Balanchine. He and other dancers saw the advantages of the Pilates method in developing strong, lean muscles without bulk.

Why Now?

After the fitness craze in the 1980s and 1990s, some exercise enthusiasts tired of aerobics and weight training. People turned to the slower, smoother Pilates method. In fact, celebrities like Madonna and Sharon Stone use the Pilates method. Professional sports teams like the Oakland Raiders have turned to the Pilates method for conditioning training.

The founder, Joseph Pilates, would be proud to know his method has regained popularity.

The Hottest Trend in Fitness

Fill in the bubble to answer each question or complete each sentence.

1. Which of these statements is true about the Pilates method?
   - Ⓐ It is based on fast aerobic exercises to strengthen the whole body.
   - Ⓑ It includes torso strengthening, stretching, balance, and breathing exercises.
   - Ⓒ To use the Pilates method, complicated equipment is needed.
   - Ⓓ Weight lifting is an integral part of the exercise program.

2. Joseph Pilates was the founder of the Pilates method. What does the word *founder* mean?
   - Ⓐ He was the first person to use the exercise program.
   - Ⓑ He found an exercise program and used it.
   - Ⓒ He found ways to get people to exercise more.
   - Ⓓ He invented the exercise program that bears his name.

3. During World War I, Joseph tested his method on _____.
   - Ⓐ wounded soldiers
   - Ⓑ enemy prisoners of war
   - Ⓒ doctors
   - Ⓓ celebrities

4. Why do dancers like the Pilate method?
   - Ⓐ They develop strong, bulky muscles.
   - Ⓑ They develop strong, lean muscles.
   - Ⓒ They are able to balance.
   - Ⓓ They are able to stretch and breathe.

5. The Pilates method is now the hottest trend in fitness. What is meant by *the hottest trend in fitness*?
   - Ⓐ It is used in homes and at fitness centers.
   - Ⓑ It is used by dancers, sports teams, and celebrities.
   - Ⓒ It is the latest craze among exercise enthusiasts.
   - Ⓓ It has been around for many years.

Bonus: On the back of this page, write a paragraph explaining why the Pilates method has become popular recently.

The Euro

Introducing the Topic

1. Reproduce page 111 for individual students, or make a transparency to use with a group or the whole class.

2. Show students the map of Europe. Point out the close proximity of the countries. Remind students that each country has its own monetary system. But as of 2002, 12 countries have joined to have a common currency. They are Austria, Belgium, Finland, France, Germany, Greece, Ireland, Italy, Luxembourg, the Netherlands, Portugal, and Spain. Ask students if they think the euro will expand beyond these borders.

Reading the Selections

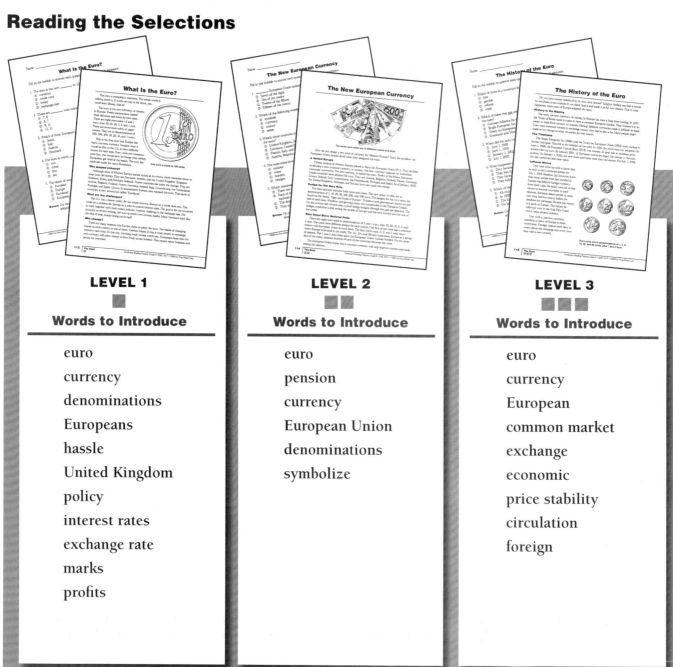

LEVEL 1

■

Words to Introduce

euro

currency

denominations

Europeans

hassle

United Kingdom

policy

interest rates

exchange rate

marks

profits

LEVEL 2

■ ■

Words to Introduce

euro

pension

currency

European Union

denominations

symbolize

LEVEL 3

■ ■ ■

Words to Introduce

euro

currency

European

common market

exchange

economic

price stability

circulation

foreign

Nonfiction Reading Practice, Grade 6 • EMC 3317 • ©2003 by Evan-Moor Corp.

Euroland—2002

Austria	France	Ireland	Netherlands
Belgium	Germany	Italy	Portugal
Finland	Greece	Luxembourg	Spain

As of 2002, the 12 European countries listed have agreed to a common currency called the euro. The euro is expanding beyond these borders each year. Which other countries do you think will join "Euroland"?

What Is the Euro?

The euro is sweeping a continent. The whole world is talking about it. If you're not hip to the latest, you could lose. Money, that is!

The euro is the new currency, or money, in Europe. Twelve nations have traded their old coins and notes for new ones. There are eight euro coins—2 and 1 euro, then 50, 20, 10, 5, 2, and 1 cent. There are seven euro notes, or paper money. They are in denominations of 500, 200, 100, 50, 20, 10, and 5 euros.

One euro is equal to 100 cents.

This is the first time that Europe has had a common currency. Imagine what it would be like in the U.S. to have different money for each state. Every time you crossed a state line, you would have to change your money. Europeans got tired of the hassle. The euro has made life easier for many Europeans.

Who jumped onboard?

Although most of Western Europe stands united in its choice, three countries chose to keep their old money. They are Denmark, Sweden, and the United Kingdom (England, Scotland, Wales, and Northern Ireland). Twelve countries did make the change. They are Austria, Belgium, Finland, France, Germany, Ireland, Italy, Luxembourg, the Netherlands, Portugal, and Spain. Greece, in southeastern Europe, also adopted the euro. This block of countries is now sometimes called "Euroland."

What are the challenges?

The U.S. has a money policy for the whole country. Europe as a whole does not. This could be a problem for Europe as it tries to control interest rates. The goal is for the countries to work together with their money policies. Another challenge is the exchange rate. For instance, as of this writing, the euro is worth two German marks. Many Germans don't like the idea of their money being cut in half!

Why change?

There are many reasons why Europe chose to adopt the euro. The hassle of changing money in each country is one of them. Another reason is that it costs money to exchange currency each time. In this way, traveling made money worth less. Europeans hope that the new currency will allow money to flow freely across borders. That means better business and profits for everyone.

Nonfiction Reading Practice, Grade 6 • EMC 3317 • ©2003 by Evan-Moor Corp.

Name _____

What Is the Euro?

Fill in the bubble to answer each question or complete each sentence.

1. The *euro* is the new _____ in 12 countries in Europe.
   - Ⓐ currency
   - Ⓑ credit card
   - Ⓒ treaty
   - Ⓓ exchange rate

2. There are _____ euro coins and _____ euro notes.
   - Ⓐ 7, 8
   - Ⓑ 8, 7
   - Ⓒ 8, 11
   - Ⓓ 11, 11

3. Which of these European countries did <u>not</u> adopt the euro?
   - Ⓐ Spain
   - Ⓑ Italy
   - Ⓒ Austria
   - Ⓓ Denmark

4. The euro is worth _____ German marks.
   - Ⓐ two
   - Ⓑ three
   - Ⓒ five
   - Ⓓ six

5. The block of countries that adopted the euro is sometimes called _____.
   - Ⓐ Euroasia
   - Ⓑ Europe
   - Ⓒ Euroland
   - Ⓓ European countries

Bonus: On the back of this page, explain why many Europeans supported the adoption of the euro.

The New European Currency

The seven euro notes are in different colors and sizes.

How do you design a new kind of currency for Western Europe? That's the problem the European Union nations faced when they designed the euro.

A United Europe

Fifteen nations of Western Europe joined to form the European Union (EU). They decided to develop a new common currency, or money. The new currency replaced the individual countries' currencies. The new currency is called the euro. Twelve of the fifteen European Union countries have adopted the euro. They are Austria, Belgium, Finland, France, Germany, Greece, Ireland, Italy, Luxembourg, the Netherlands, Portugal, and Spain. As of January 2003, the United Kingdom, Denmark, and Sweden have not made the change.

Design for the Euro Note

The euro actually includes both notes and coins. The new notes, or bills, are in denominations of 5, 10, 20, 50, 100, 200, and 500 euro. The designs for the euro notes are based on the theme "Ages and Styles of Europe." Windows and gateways are shown on one side of each note. Windows and gateways show the cooperation in the European Union. On the reverse side of each note, typical bridge designs through the ages are depicted. The bridges symbolize a link among the people of Europe and between Europe and the rest of the world.

Euro Coins Show National Pride

There are eight euro coins in denominations of 2 and 1 euro, then 50, 20, 10, 5, 2, and 1 cent. The coins have different designs for each nation. One face of the coins has a common theme—the European Union in some form. The first three coins (1, 2, and 5 cent) show where Europe is located in the world. The 10-, 20-, and 50-cent coins show Europe as a group of nations. The 1 and 2 euro coins show the European Union without borders. On the other face of the coins, national symbols of each of the countries decorate the coins.

The European Union hopes that a common currency will help improve tourism and trade among the nations.

Name _____

The New European Currency

Fill in the bubble to answer each question or complete the sentence.

1. _____ European Union nations have adopted the euro.
   Ⓐ Seven of the eight
   Ⓑ Ten of the twelve
   Ⓒ Twelve of the fifteen
   Ⓓ Fifteen of the twenty

2. Which of the following words does <u>not</u> describe the euro?
   Ⓐ symbols
   Ⓑ currency
   Ⓒ money
   Ⓓ notes

3. Which three countries in Western Europe have <u>not</u> made the switch to the euro?
   Ⓐ United Kingdom, Denmark, and Sweden
   Ⓑ Germany, United Kingdom, and Denmark
   Ⓒ France, Italy, and Spain
   Ⓓ Austria, Belgium, and Germany

4. The euro notes show designs of windows, gateways, and _____.
   Ⓐ nations
   Ⓑ maps
   Ⓒ borders
   Ⓓ bridges

5. Which statement is true about euro coins?
   Ⓐ There are seven euro coins.
   Ⓑ Each of the countries designed the coins with their particular national symbols.
   Ⓒ The designs are based on the theme "Ages and Styles of Europe."
   Ⓓ They are in denominations of 5, 10, 20, 50, 100, 200, and 500 euro.

Bonus: On the back of this page, compare the euro coins to U.S. coins. How are they alike and how are they different?

The History of the Euro

Do you have money hidden away in your sock drawer? Imagine finding out that it would be worthless in six months if you didn't find it and trade it in for new money. That is what happened when most of Europe adopted the euro.

History in the Making

The euro, the new currency, or money, in Europe has been a long time coming. In 1957, the Treaty of Rome made it a goal to have a common European market. They wanted it to be easier to trade from country to country. Having different currencies made it difficult to trade. Every time someone wanted to exchange money, they had to pay a fee. Many people didn't trade or buy things in other countries for this reason.

The Timetable

The Single European Act (1986) and the Treaty on European Union (1992) both worked to further this goal. This led to the creation of the euro. In 1995, the name *euro* was adopted. On June 1, 1998, the European Central Bank (ECB) was created. Its goal was to maintain price stability for the euro. By January 2001, 12 European countries began the change to the euro system. On January 1, 2002, the new coins and notes went into circulation. On July 1, 2002, the old currencies lost their value.

Leftover Money

One man came up with a clever idea to cash in old currencies before the July 1, 2002 deadline. Jay Sorenson knew that many people who had traveled to Europe had leftover foreign currency from their trips. He didn't want all of that money to become souvenirs in sock drawers. Sorenson asked people to send him their leftover money before the deadline for exchange. He sent the money to a bank in Europe. The money he collected went to the Kids First Fund, which helps abused children.

Now with a common currency, traveling in parts of Europe is more convenient. Foreign visitors don't have to worry about the exchange rate every time they visit a new country.

Euro coins are in denominations of 1, 2, 5, 10, 20, and 50 cents, plus 1 and 2 euro.

Name _____

The History of the Euro

Fill in the bubble to answer each question or complete each sentence.

1. Which of these is a synonym for the word *exchange*?
   - Ⓐ lose
   - Ⓑ gamble
   - Ⓒ refund
   - Ⓓ trade

2. Which of these was <u>not</u> one of the treaties that led to the adoption of the euro?
   - Ⓐ German Alliance for the Deutschmark
   - Ⓑ Single European Act
   - Ⓒ Treaty on European Union
   - Ⓓ Economic and Monetary Union

3. When did the euro coins go into circulation?
   - Ⓐ June 1, 1998
   - Ⓑ June 1, 1999
   - Ⓒ January 1, 2002
   - Ⓓ July 1, 2002

4. What happened to old currencies after the adoption of the euro?
   - Ⓐ They became more valuable.
   - Ⓑ They lost their value.
   - Ⓒ They became illegal.
   - Ⓓ They held their value and are still in circulation.

5. Which of these statements is true about the euro?
   - Ⓐ All countries in Europe have adopted the euro.
   - Ⓑ In 1999, the name *euro* was adopted.
   - Ⓒ The European Central Bank handles all euro transactions.
   - Ⓓ On January 1, 2002, the euro coins and notes went into circulation.

Bonus: On the back of this page, write a newspaper story about Jay Sorenson and his clever plan to help kids.

Investing for the Future

Introducing the Topic

1. Reproduce page 119 for individual students, or make a transparency to use with a group or the whole class.

2. Ask students how many of them have a savings account. Then ask students how many of them play the stock market. Show students four ways to save or invest and ask them which one they think will yield them the highest return.

Reading the Selections

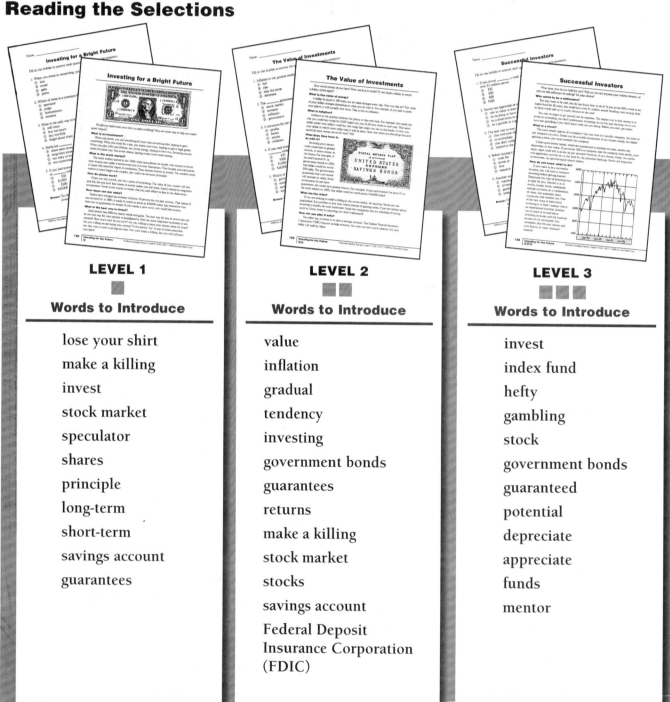

LEVEL 1

Words to Introduce

lose your shirt

make a killing

invest

stock market

speculator

shares

principle

long-term

short-term

savings account

guarantees

LEVEL 2

Words to Introduce

value

inflation

gradual

tendency

investing

government bonds

guarantees

returns

make a killing

stock market

stocks

savings account

Federal Deposit
Insurance Corporation
(FDIC)

LEVEL 3

Words to Introduce

invest

index fund

hefty

gambling

stock

government bonds

guaranteed

potential

depreciate

appreciate

funds

mentor

Nonfiction Reading Practice, Grade 6 • EMC 3317 • ©2003 by Evan-Moor Corp.

Ways to Invest for the Future

Which of the following ways of investing your money will give you the highest return?

1. One way to invest in your future is to save your money in a piggy bank.

2. Another way to invest in your future is to put money into a savings account.

3. A third way to invest in your future is to buy U.S. government bonds.

4. A fourth way to invest in your future is to play the stock market.

Investing for a Bright Future

Would you rather lose your shirt or make a killing? Here are some tips to help you make good choices!

What is an investment?

When you invest, you put something of yours into something else, hoping to gain something. When you study for a test, you invest your time, hoping to gain a high grade. When you play with your friends, you invest energy, hoping to have fun. Investing money works the same way. You invest money, hoping to earn even more money.

What is the stock market?

The stock market started in the 1700s when speculators, or people who wanted to invest their money, met under a buttonwood tree in Lower Manhattan. They bought and sold pieces of paper that stood for shares in companies. They became known as stocks. The modern stock market is much bigger and complex, but works on the same principle.

How do stocks work?

When you buy a stock, you buy a piece of something. The value of your stocks will rise and fall, but you can't lose money in stocks unless you sell them. Stocks should be long-term investments. Never invest money in stocks that you can't afford to lose in the short-term.

How much can you make?

Stocks have averaged an increase of almost 10 percent for the past century. That means if you invested $1 in 1900, it could be worth as much as $10,000 today. Just remember that there are no guarantees on stocks. If you choose a poor stock, you could lose money.

What is the best way to invest?

Each person has different money needs and goals. The best way for you to invest may not be the best way for your parents or grandparents. Here are some important questions to ask yourself: How much time do you have? Are you willing to leave your money alone for years? Are you willing to risk losing your money? If you answer "no" to any of these questions, you may want to start a savings account. You won't make a killing, but you will still have your shirt!

Name _____

Investing for a Bright Future

Fill in the bubble to answer each question or complete the sentence.

1. When you *invest* in something, you hope to _____ something.
   - Ⓐ lose
   - Ⓑ avoid
   - Ⓒ gain
   - Ⓓ prove

2. Which of these is a synonym for a *speculator*?
   - Ⓐ spectator
   - Ⓑ judge
   - Ⓒ businessman
   - Ⓓ investor

3. What is the only way to lose money in stocks?
   - Ⓐ sell them
   - Ⓑ buy too much
   - Ⓒ buy too little
   - Ⓓ forget about them

4. *Stocks* are _____.
   - Ⓐ short-term investments
   - Ⓑ long-term investments
   - Ⓒ too risky to buy
   - Ⓓ too conservative to buy

5. If you had invested $1 in stocks in 1900, it could be worth as much as _____ today.
   - Ⓐ $50
   - Ⓑ $1,000
   - Ⓒ $500
   - Ⓓ $10,000

Bonus: On the back of this page, explain why you might have different investing goals than your parents.

The Value of Investments

How much money do you have? How much is it worth? If you think a dollar is worth a dollar, think again!

What is the value of money?

A dollar is equal to 100 cents, but its value changes every day. How can this be? The value of your dollar changes depending on what you do with it. For example, if you hide it under your pillow, it will actually lose value. This is due to inflation.

What is inflation?

Inflation is the gradual tendency for prices to rise over time. For example, the candy bar that you could buy today for $1.00 might cost you $1.10 next week or next year. That same dollar under your pillow could buy the candy bar today, but not in the future. In this way, your dollar is worth more today than it will be later. Does that mean you should go out and spend all your money on candy bars? NO!

What does time have to do with it?

Investing your money today could lead to greater returns, or more money, in the future. For example, if you had invested $1 in government bonds in 1900, that dollar would be worth $50 today. The government guarantees that your bonds will increase in value. Some investments do not have guarantees, but could earn greater returns. For example, if you had invested the same $1 in the stock market in 1900, that dollar could be worth about $10,000 today!

What are the risks?

If you are looking to make a killing in the stock market, be cautious. Stocks are not guaranteed. It is possible to lose your money instead of gaining more. If you are serious about investing in stocks, do your homework. Study the companies you are thinking of buying stock in. Never invest in anything you don't understand!

How can you play it safe?

The safest way to invest is to open a savings account. The Federal Deposit Insurance Corporation (FDIC) insures savings accounts. You may not earn much interest, but your dollar will hold its value.

Nonfiction Reading Practice, Grade 6 • EMC 3317 • ©2003 by Evan-Moor Corp.

Name _____

The Value of Investments

Fill in the bubble to answer the question or complete each sentence.

1. *Inflation* is the gradual tendency of prices to _____ over time.
   - Ⓐ fall
   - Ⓑ rise
   - Ⓒ stay the same
   - Ⓓ decrease

2. The _____ guarantees that your bonds will increase in value.
   - Ⓐ stock market
   - Ⓑ investor
   - Ⓒ inflation
   - Ⓓ government

3. A synonym for the word *returns* is _____.
   - Ⓐ profits
   - Ⓑ losses
   - Ⓒ stocks
   - Ⓓ inflation

4. If you had invested $1 in government bonds in 1900, it could be worth about _____ today.
   - Ⓐ $50
   - Ⓑ $500
   - Ⓒ $1,000
   - Ⓓ $10,000

5. Which of these is insured by the FDIC?
   - Ⓐ government bonds
   - Ⓑ stocks
   - Ⓒ savings accounts
   - Ⓓ lottery tickets

Bonus: On the back of this page, explain why it is risky to invest in the stock market.

Successful Investors

What does your future hold for you? Will you be rich beyond your wildest dreams, or will the bill collectors be calling? It's your choice!

Who wants to be a millionaire?

You may want to be rich, but do you know how to do it? If you invest $20 a week in an index fund for 40 years, you could have over $1 million saved! Building your savings little by little could add up to a hefty fortune in the end!

You may be eager to get started, but be cautious. The easiest way to lose money is to invest in something you don't understand. Investing can be fun and exciting, but it can turn into gambling if you don't know what you are doing. Before you start, get smart.

What is a stock?

The more stocks (pieces of a company) that you own of a specific company, the more of the company you own. Stocks can be a terrific investment if you choose wisely, but before picking a stock, you must research the company.

Unlike government bonds, which are guaranteed to increase in value, stocks may depreciate, or lose value. If you invest $20 in a company and the company does poorly, your stock value could fall to as low as just pennies! However, if you choose wisely, the stocks will appreciate, and the sky is the limit for the potential earnings. Stocks are long-term investments, not get-rich-quick lottery tickets.

How do you know what to do?

If you want to be a successful investor, you will have to research investing before getting started. Determine the type of investing that is right for you, whether it is in stocks, bonds, funds, traditional savings accounts, or a combination of these. Ask questions about companies that interest you. One of the best ways to learn about investing is to find a mentor who is an experienced investor. Another way to learn is to read about investing in books and the business section of the newspaper. Just remember that it's your money and your future, so make educated choices!

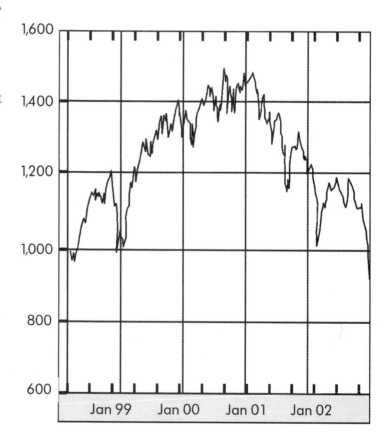

Name _____

Successful Investors

Fill in the bubble to answer each question or complete each sentence.

1. If you invest _____ a week in an index fund for 40 years, you could have over $1 million saved.
   - Ⓐ $10
   - Ⓑ $20
   - Ⓒ $50
   - Ⓓ $100

2. Stocks can *appreciate* or *depreciate* in value. This means stocks can _____.
   - Ⓐ rise in value or lose their value
   - Ⓑ be limiting or have potential
   - Ⓒ be a short-term or a long-term investment
   - Ⓓ be a gamble or a get-rich-quick investment

3. The best way to lose money is to invest in something _____.
   - Ⓐ that everyone else is buying
   - Ⓑ in technology
   - Ⓒ you don't understand
   - Ⓓ related to the food industry

4. Before buying a stock, you must _____ the company.
   - Ⓐ work for
   - Ⓑ invest in
   - Ⓒ love
   - Ⓓ research

5. Another word for *mentor* is _____.
   - Ⓐ teacher
   - Ⓑ investor
   - Ⓒ gambler
   - Ⓓ index fund

Bonus: On the back of this page, write which kind of investment choice you would make if you had $1,000. Would you choose playing the stock market, buying government bonds, or putting it in a savings account?

Measuring Time

Introducing the Topic

1. Reproduce page 127 for individual students, or make a transparency to use with a group or the whole class.

2. Have students look at the school clock to check the time. Ask them if they know what time it is across the country from them. Share with students the U.S. time zone map. Read and practice calculating times in different zones.

Reading the Selections

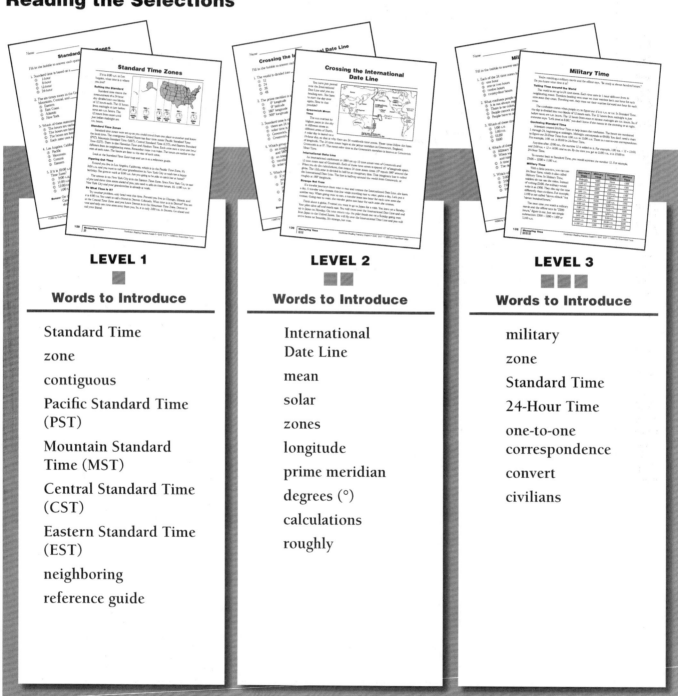

LEVEL 1
■

Words to Introduce

Standard Time

zone

contiguous

Pacific Standard Time (PST)

Mountain Standard Time (MST)

Central Standard Time (CST)

Eastern Standard Time (EST)

neighboring

reference guide

LEVEL 2
■ ■

Words to Introduce

International Date Line

mean

solar

zones

longitude

prime meridian

degrees (°)

calculations

roughly

LEVEL 3
■ ■ ■

Words to Introduce

military

zone

Standard Time

24-Hour Time

one-to-one correspondence

convert

civilians

Nonfiction Reading Practice, Grade 6 • EMC 3317 • ©2003 by Evan-Moor Corp.

United States Time Zones

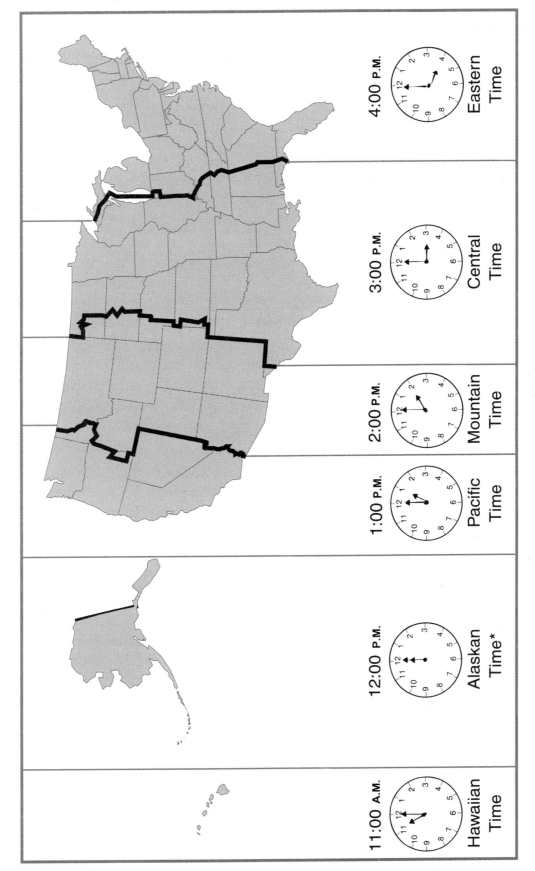

4:00 P.M. Eastern Time

3:00 P.M. Central Time

2:00 P.M. Mountain Time

1:00 P.M. Pacific Time

12:00 P.M. Alaskan Time*

11:00 A.M. Hawaiian Time

*Note: Alaska is divided into several time zones, only one of which is shown here.

Standard Time Zones

If it is 8:00 A.M. in Los Angeles, what time is it where you live?

Setting the Standard

Standard time means the measurement of a 24-hour day divided into two blocks of 12 hours each. The 12 hours from midnight to just before noon are A.M. hours. The 12 hours from noon until just before midnight are P.M. hours.

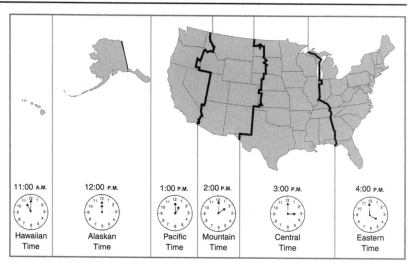

| 11:00 A.M. | 12:00 P.M. | 1:00 P.M. | 2:00 P.M. | 3:00 P.M. | 4:00 P.M. |
| Hawaiian Time | Alaskan Time | Pacific Time | Mountain Time | Central Time | Eastern Time |

Standard Time Zones

Standard time zones were set up so you could travel from one place to another and know the local time. The contiguous United States has four time zones: Pacific Standard Time (PST), Mountain Standard Time (MST), Central Standard Time (CST), and Eastern Standard Time (EST). There is also Hawaiian Time and Alaskan Time. Each zone uses a time one hour different from its neighboring zones. Remember these two rules: The hours are earlier to the west of each zone. The hours are later to the east of each zone.

Look at the Standard Time Zone map and use it as a reference guide.

Figuring Out Time

Pretend you live in Los Angeles, California, which is in the Pacific Time Zone. It's 8:00 A.M. and you want to call your grandmother in New York City to wish her a happy birthday. She goes to work at 9:00 A.M. Are you going to be able to catch her at home?

The answer is no. New York City is in the Eastern Time Zone. Since New York City is east of you and three time zones ahead of you, you need to add on three hours. It's 11:00 A.M. in New York City and your grandmother is already at work.

So What Time Is It?

Try another problem, only head west this time. Pretend you live in Chicago, Illinois, and it is 4:00 P.M. You want to call a friend in Denver, Colorado. What time is it in Denver? You are in the Central Time Zone, and you know Denver is in the Mountain Time Zone. Denver is west and only one time zone away from you. So, it is only 3:00 P.M. in Denver. Go ahead and call your friend.

Nonfiction Reading Practice, Grade 6 • EMC 3317 • ©2003 by Evan-Moor Corp.

Name _____

Standard Time Zones

Fill in the bubble to answer each question or complete each sentence.

1. Standard time is based on a _____ day.
   - Ⓐ 1-hour
   - Ⓑ 6-hour
   - Ⓒ 12-hour
   - Ⓓ 24-hour

2. The six times zones in the United States are called Hawaiian, Alaskan, Pacific, Mountain, Central, and _____ zones.
   - Ⓐ Eastern
   - Ⓑ East Coast
   - Ⓒ Atlantic
   - Ⓓ New York

3. Which of these statements is true about Standard Time Zones?
   - Ⓐ The hours are earlier to the east of each zone.
   - Ⓑ The hours are later to the east of each zone.
   - Ⓒ The hours are later to the west of each zone.
   - Ⓓ Each zone uses a time two hours different from its neighboring zones.

4. Los Angeles, California, is in the _____ Time Zone.
   - Ⓐ Pacific
   - Ⓑ Mountain
   - Ⓒ Central
   - Ⓓ Eastern

5. If it is 10:00 A.M. in the Mountain Time Zone, what time is it in the Eastern Time Zone?
   - Ⓐ 9:00 A.M.
   - Ⓑ 11:00 A.M.
   - Ⓒ 12:00 P.M.
   - Ⓓ 1:00 P.M.

Bonus: On the back of this page, figure out what time it is in Iowa and South Carolina if it is 2:00 P.M. in Seattle, Washington. Draw three clocks showing the correct times in Alaska, Hawaii, and Washington.

Crossing the International Date Line

You have just passed over the International Date Line and you are heading east. You have to start the day over again. How is that possible?

Greenwich Mean Time

The sun reaches its highest point in the sky at different times in different areas of Earth. A solar day is based on a

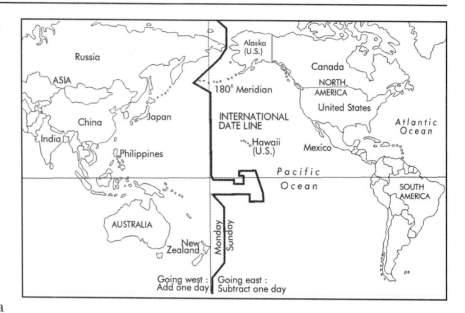

24-hour day, so that is why there are 24 worldwide time zones. These times follow the lines of longitude. The 24 time zones begin at the prime meridian in Greenwich, England. Greenwich is at 0°. The mean solar time at the Greenwich meridian is known as Greenwich Mean Time.

International Date Line

An international conference in 1884 set up 12 time zones west of Greenwich and 12 time zones east of Greenwich. Each of those time zones is spaced 15° of longitude apart. When you do the calculations, that means 24 time zones times 15° equals 360° around the globe. The 12th zone is divided in half by an imaginary line. This imaginary line is called the International Date Line. The line is halfway around the world from Greenwich, or roughly at 180° longitude.

Strange But True

If a traveler journeys from west to east and crosses the International Date Line, she loses a day. A traveler who crosses this line while traveling east to west, gains a day. Let's put it another way. When going west to east, a traveler loses one hour for each time zone she crosses. Going east to west, the traveler gains one hour for each zone she crosses.

Think about a globe. Pretend you want to go to Japan for a visit. You leave on a Sunday. Your pilot takes off and heads east. You will cross over the International Date Line and end up in Japan on Monday. On your return trip, the pilot heads out on a Sunday going west from Japan to the United States. You will fly over the International Date Line and you will arrive home on Saturday. It's strange, but true.

Nonfiction Reading Practice, Grade 6 • EMC 3317 • ©2003 by Evan-Moor Corp.

Name _____

Crossing the International Date Line

Fill in the bubble to answer each question or complete each sentence.

1. The world is divided into _____ time zones.
   - Ⓐ 12
   - Ⓑ 24
   - Ⓒ 36
   - Ⓓ 48

2. The *prime meridian* is an imaginary line located at _____.
   - Ⓐ 0° longitude
   - Ⓑ 0° latitude
   - Ⓒ 180° longitude
   - Ⓓ 360° longitude

3. Standard time is called *Greenwich Mean Time* because _____.
   - Ⓐ there are 24 times zones
   - Ⓑ solar time is measured in degrees
   - Ⓒ Greenwich, England, is located at the prime meridian
   - Ⓓ Greenwich, England, is located at the International Date Line

4. Which group of phrases best describes the International Date Line?
   - Ⓐ an imaginary line, halfway around the world from Greenwich, and 180°
   - Ⓑ an imaginary line, prime meridian, and date line
   - Ⓒ traveling east, traveling west, traveling south, and traveling north
   - Ⓓ solar time, measured in 15° segments, and 24 hours in a day

5. Which of these statements is true about the International Date Line?
   - Ⓐ If you go from west to east and cross the International Date Line, you gain a day.
   - Ⓑ If you go from east to west and cross the International Date Line, you lose a day.
   - Ⓒ If you go from east to west and cross the International Date Line, you gain a day.
   - Ⓓ It does not matter which direction you go, you will always lose a day.

Bonus: On the back of this page, explain how crossing the International Date Line affects travel plans.

Military Time

You're watching a military movie and the officer says, "Be ready at eleven hundred hours." Do you know what time it is?

Telling Time Around the World

The world is set up in 24 time zones. Each time zone is 1 hour different from its neighboring zones. Travelers heading west must set their watches back one hour for each time zone they cross. Traveling east, they must set their watches forward one hour for each zone.

The confusion comes when people try to figure out if it is A.M. or P.M. In Standard Time, the day is divided into two blocks of 12 hours each. The 12 hours from midnight to just before noon are A.M. hours. The 12 hours from noon to almost midnight are P.M. hours. So, if someone says, "Let's meet at 8:00," you don't know if she means in the morning or at night.

Confusing Standard Time

Scientists created 24-Hour Time to help lessen the confusion. The hours are numbered 1 through 24, beginning at midnight. Midnight corresponds to 00:00. You don't need a chart to figure out 24-Hour Time from 1:00 A.M. to 11:00 A.M. There is a one-to-one correspondence. For example, 1:00 A.M. is 01:00 in 24-Hour Time.

Anytime after 12:00 P.M., the number 12 is added to it. For example, 1:00 P.M. + 12 = 13:00, and 2:00 P.M. + 12 = 14:00, and so on. By the time you get to 11:00 P.M., it is 23:00 in 24-Hour Time.

To convert back to Standard Time, you would subtract the number 12. For example, 23:00 − 12:00 = 11:00 A.M.

Military Time

With a little practice, you can use 24-Hour Time, which is also called Military Time. In Military Time, soldiers do not use the colon. Instead of writing 23:00, the military would write it as 2300. They also say the time differently than civilians. For example, 11:00 is not called "eleven o'clock" but "eleven hundred hours."

The next time you watch a military movie and the officer says its "2300 hours," figure it out. Just use simple subtraction: 2300 − 1200 = 1100 or 11:00 A.M.

Standard Time	Military Time	Standard Time	Military Time
Midnight	0000	Noon	1200
1:00 A.M.	0100	1:00 P.M.	1300
2:00 A.M.	0200	2:00 P.M.	1400
3:00 A.M.	0300	3:00 P.M.	1500
4:00 A.M.	0400	4:00 P.M.	1600
5:00 A.M.	0500	5:00 P.M.	1700
6:00 A.M.	0600	6:00 P.M.	1800
7:00 A.M.	0700	7:00 P.M.	1900
8:00 A.M.	0800	8:00 P.M.	2000
9:00 A.M.	0900	9:00 P.M.	2100
10:00 A.M.	1000	10:00 P.M.	2200
11:00 A.M.	1100	11:00 P.M.	2300

Nonfiction Reading Practice, Grade 6 • EMC 3317 • ©2003 by Evan-Moor Corp.

Name _____

Military Time

Fill in the bubble to answer each question or complete each sentence.

1. Each of the 24 time zones is _____ different from its neighboring zones.
   - Ⓐ one hour
   - Ⓑ one or two hours
   - Ⓒ twelve hours
   - Ⓓ twenty-four hours

2. What confuses people about Standard Time?
   - Ⓐ It is not always regularly used.
   - Ⓑ There is no colon, so it is hard to read hours and minutes.
   - Ⓒ People cannot simply say a time without adding A.M. or P.M.
   - Ⓓ People have to add or subtract the number 12 all the time.

3. Which of these times is an example of 24-Hour Time?
   - Ⓐ 1:00 A.M.
   - Ⓑ 1:00 P.M.
   - Ⓒ 01:00
   - Ⓓ 0100

4. Which of these statements is <u>not</u> true about Military Time?
   - Ⓐ Military Time is about the same as 24-Hour Time.
   - Ⓑ When writing the time of day, a colon is placed between the hour and minutes.
   - Ⓒ A time such as 10:00 A.M. would be stated as "ten hundred hours."
   - Ⓓ The number 12 is needed to convert civilian time to military time.

5. Which of these examples shows a *one-to-one correspondence*?
   - Ⓐ 3:00 to 15:00
   - Ⓑ 5:00 A.M. to 5:00 P.M.
   - Ⓒ 7:00 P.M. to 1900
   - Ⓓ 9:00 A.M. to 09:00

Bonus: On the back of this page, make up three math problems to solve using Military Time. Be sure to include the answers to the problems. Try them out on a friend.

Jazz

Introducing the Topic

1. Reproduce page 135 for individual students, or make a transparency to use with a group or the whole class.

2. Ask students to name their favorite style of music. They will probably name styles such as rap or rock and roll. Tell students they are going to read about jazz, a kind of music that originated in the United States in the late 1800s. Share with them the picture of a jazz band and discuss the different kinds of instruments that are commonly found in jazz.

Reading the Selections

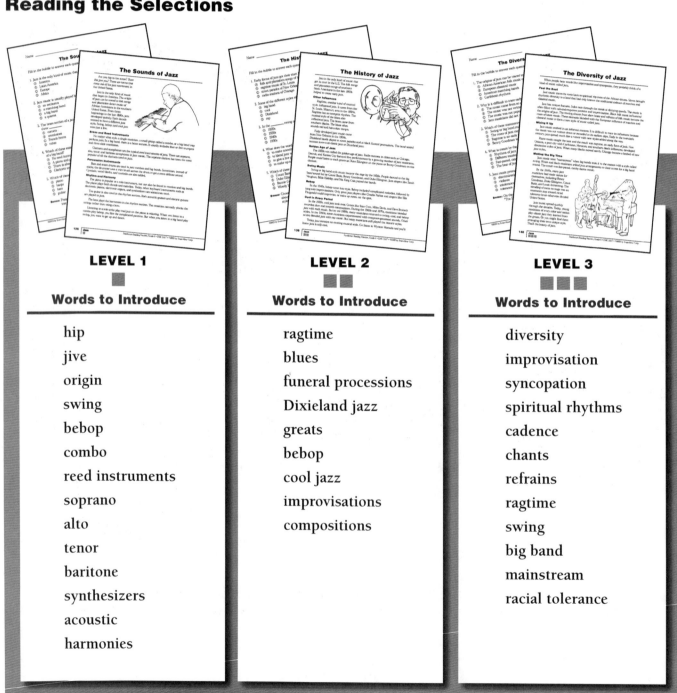

LEVEL 1
Words to Introduce

hip

jive

origin

swing

bebop

combo

reed instruments

soprano

alto

tenor

baritone

synthesizers

acoustic

harmonies

LEVEL 2
Words to Introduce

ragtime

blues

funeral processions

Dixieland jazz

greats

bebop

cool jazz

improvisations

compositions

LEVEL 3
Words to Introduce

diversity

improvisation

syncopation

spiritual rhythms

cadence

chants

refrains

ragtime

swing

big band

mainstream

racial tolerance

Traditional Jazz Band Instruments

In a traditional jazz band, there is a front line of musicians that play a trumpet, trombone, and a clarinet or saxophone. The rhythm section consists of a bass, a piano, and often a guitar.

The Sounds of Jazz

Are you hip to the scene? Does this jive you? These are terms that came out of the jazz movement in the United States.

Jazz is the only kind of music that began in America. The origin of jazz can be traced to folk songs and plantation dance music of African Americans in the southern United States. From those beginnings in the late 1800s, jazz developed quickly. Each decade seemed to have a different jazz style. Swing, bebop, and cool jazz were just a few.

Brass and Reed Instruments

No matter what style, a single musician, a small group called a combo, or a big band may perform jazz. In a big band, there is a brass section. It usually includes four or five trumpets and three slide trombones.

Clarinets and saxophones are the typical reed instruments of jazz. There are soprano, alto, tenor, and baritone saxophones in jazz music. The soprano clarinet has been the most popular of all the clarinets used in jazz.

Percussion Instruments

Bass and snare drums are used in jazz combos and big bands. Sometimes, instead of sticks, the drummer uses a wire brush across the drum to get a more delicate sound. Cymbals, wood blocks, and cowbells are also added.

Rhythm and Harmony

The piano is popular as a solo instrument, but can also be found in combos and big bands. The piano plays both chords and melodies. Today, other keyboard instruments such as electronic pianos, electronic organs, and synthesizers are sometimes used.

The guitar is also used in the rhythm section. Both acoustic guitars and electric guitars are played in jazz.

The bass plays the harmonies in the rhythm section. The musician normally plucks the strings rather than using a bow.

Listening to a solo artist play cool jazz on the piano is relaxing. When you listen to a combo play bebop, you like the complicated patterns. But when you listen to a big band play swing, you want to get up and dance.

Nonfiction Reading Practice, Grade 6 • EMC 3317 • ©2003 by Evan-Moor Corp.

The Sounds of Jazz

Fill in the bubble to answer each question or complete each statement.

1. Jazz is the only kind of music that originated in _____.
   Ⓐ America
   Ⓑ Latin America
   Ⓒ Europe
   Ⓓ Africa

2. Jazz music is usually played by a solo musician, a small combo, or in _____.
   Ⓐ an orchestra
   Ⓑ a marching band
   Ⓒ a big band
   Ⓓ a quartet

3. The brass section of a jazz big band consists of four or five trumpets and three _____.
   Ⓐ cornets
   Ⓑ trombones
   Ⓒ French horns
   Ⓓ tubas

4. Which of these statements is true about the instruments in the reed section of a big band?
   Ⓐ No reed instruments are played in a big band.
   Ⓑ A piano and guitar round out the reed section.
   Ⓒ There is always a bass playing in the background.
   Ⓓ Clarinets and saxophones are common reed instruments.

5. Which of these instruments was <u>not</u> mentioned in this article?
   Ⓐ piano
   Ⓑ banjo
   Ⓒ bass
   Ⓓ guitar

Bonus: Pretend you are in a jazz band. On the back of this sheet, name what instrument you play and why you like it so much.

The History of Jazz

Jazz is the only kind of music that got its start in the U.S. The folk songs and plantation songs of southern black Americans in the late 1800s helped to create early jazz.

Other Influences

Ragtime, another kind of musical style, influenced jazz. It came from the St. Louis, Missouri, area in the 1890s. Ragtime has an energetic rhythm. The musical style of the blues also influenced jazz. The blues came from southern blacks. The blues often sounds sad and has a slow tempo.

Fully developed jazz music came from New Orleans in the 1900s. Dixieland bands played at street parades and at black funeral processions. The band sound became known as classic jazz or Dixieland jazz.

Golden Age of Jazz

The 1920s was called the golden age of jazz. Radio stations in cities such as Chicago, Detroit, and Kansas City featured live performances by a growing number of jazz musicians. People could listen to such greats as Duke Ellington on the piano or Benny Goodman on the clarinet.

Swing Music

Swing or big band style music became the rage by the 1930s. People danced to the big band sound led by Count Basie, Benny Goodman, and Duke Ellington. Jazz singers like Sarah Vaughan, Billie Holiday, and Nat King Cole joined the bands.

Bebop

In the 1940s, bebop came into style. Bebop included complicated melodies, followed by long solo improvisations. Only great jazz players like Charlie Parker and singers like Ella Fitzgerald could improvise, or make up notes, on the spot.

Cool in Every Period

In the 1950s, cool jazz took over. Greats like Stan Getz, Miles Davis, and Dave Brubeck recorded slow and smooth compositions. During the 1960s and 1970s, musicians blended jazz with rock music. But by the 1980s, many musicians returned to swing, cool, and bebop styles. In the 1990s, some musicians experimented with computer-generated sounds. Other artists blended jazz with rap music. But many musicians still played the historic styles.

Today, jazz remains an exciting musical style. Go listen to Wynton Marsalis and you'll know jazz is still cool.

Nonfiction Reading Practice, Grade 6 • EMC 3317 • ©2003 by Evan-Moor Corp.

Name _____

The History of Jazz

Fill in the bubble to answer each question or complete each sentence.

1. Early forms of jazz got their start in the _____.
   - Ⓐ folk and plantation songs of black Americans of the South
   - Ⓑ ragtime music of St. Louis
   - Ⓒ street parades of New Orleans
   - Ⓓ radio stations of Chicago

2. Some of the different styles of jazz include classic, swing, bebop, and _____.
   - Ⓐ big band
   - Ⓑ cool
   - Ⓒ Dixieland
   - Ⓓ rap

3. In the _____, swing or big band music became the rage.
   - Ⓐ 1920s
   - Ⓑ 1930s
   - Ⓒ 1940s
   - Ⓓ 1950s

4. What does the word *improvise* mean as used in this article?
   - Ⓐ to make smooth compositions
   - Ⓑ to blend jazz with other styles of music
   - Ⓒ to give a live performance
   - Ⓓ to make up original music on the spot

5. Which of these big band leaders was <u>not</u> mentioned in the article?
   - Ⓐ Count Basie
   - Ⓑ Duke Ellington
   - Ⓒ Bennie Goodman
   - Ⓓ Woody Herman

Bonus: Choose your favorite time period of jazz. On the back of this page, write about what made that period of jazz important. Be sure to include names, styles, and why you like it.

The Diversity of Jazz

When people hear words like *improvisation* and *syncopation*, they probably think of a kind of music called jazz.

Feel the Beat

Jazz music traces its roots back to spiritual rhythms of the African drums. Slaves brought rhythmic diversity to a land that had only known the traditional cadence of marches and classical music.

Jazz has unique features. Solos race through the music at dizzying speeds. The music is often filled with call-and-response patterns and improvisation. Black folk music influenced the origins of jazz. The rowing chants from slave boats and refrains of folk music became the roots of blues music. These elements blended with the European influence of marches and classical music to form a new style of music called jazz.

Mixing It Up

Jazz music evolved in an informal manner. It is difficult to trace its influences because the music was not written down or recorded in its earliest days. Early in the twentieth century, jazz spread much like a rumor with new styles added along the way.

Piano music caught the beat and the result was ragtime, an early form of jazz. New Orleans, a port city with Caribbean, Mexican, and southern black influences, developed distinctive styles of jazz. When many blacks moved north, Chicago became a hotbed of new jazz styles.

Making the Big Time

Jazz music went "mainstream" when big bands took it to the masses with a style called swing. White and black musicians added jazz arrangements to their scores for a big band sound. The result was fast-paced, catchy dance music.

By the 1940s, many jazz musicians had made names for themselves, including Benny Goodman, Duke Ellington, Count Basie, and Louis Armstrong. The blending of races on stage was an enormous step toward racial tolerance in an otherwise divided United States.

Jazz music spread quickly through the decades. Today, young musicians of every color and nation play classic jazz they learned from the greats. Or you might find them arranging their own unique style. That's the beauty of jazz.

Nonfiction Reading Practice, Grade 6 • EMC 3317 • ©2003 by Evan-Moor Corp.

Name _____

The Diversity of Jazz

Fill in the bubble to answer each question or complete each sentence.

1. The origins of jazz can be traced to _____.
   - Ⓐ African American folk music of the South
   - Ⓑ European classical music
   - Ⓒ American marching bands
   - Ⓓ Caribbean rhythms

2. Why is it difficult to trace early influences of jazz music?
   - Ⓐ The music came from so many different countries.
   - Ⓑ The music was not written down or recorded.
   - Ⓒ The music was not popular, so people did not pay attention to it.
   - Ⓓ Jazz musicians did not want to share their original compositions.

3. Which of these statements is true about jazz?
   - Ⓐ Swing or big band music is the only style of jazz.
   - Ⓑ The roots of jazz can be traced to the city of Chicago.
   - Ⓒ Ragtime is an early style of jazz that is often played on the piano.
   - Ⓓ Benny Goodman was the best swing bandleader.

4. What is meant by the term *rhythmic diversity* as used in this article?
   - Ⓐ Rhythms of jazz come from African drums.
   - Ⓑ Different musical patterns and styles came from a variety of sources.
   - Ⓒ Fast-paced, catchy music was unique to jazz.
   - Ⓓ The beat of jazz was influenced by European classical music.

5. Jazz music promoted racial _____.
   - Ⓐ discrimination
   - Ⓑ violence
   - Ⓒ intolerance
   - Ⓓ tolerance

Bonus: On the back of this page, write why the title of this article is called "The Diversity of Jazz."

Special Effects

Introducing the Topic

1. Reproduce page 143 for individual students, or make a transparency to use with a group or the whole class.

2. Ask students to think about movies they have seen that used special effects. Show students the four examples of special effects techniques. Read and discuss different movies they have seen that used those four techniques.

Reading the Selections

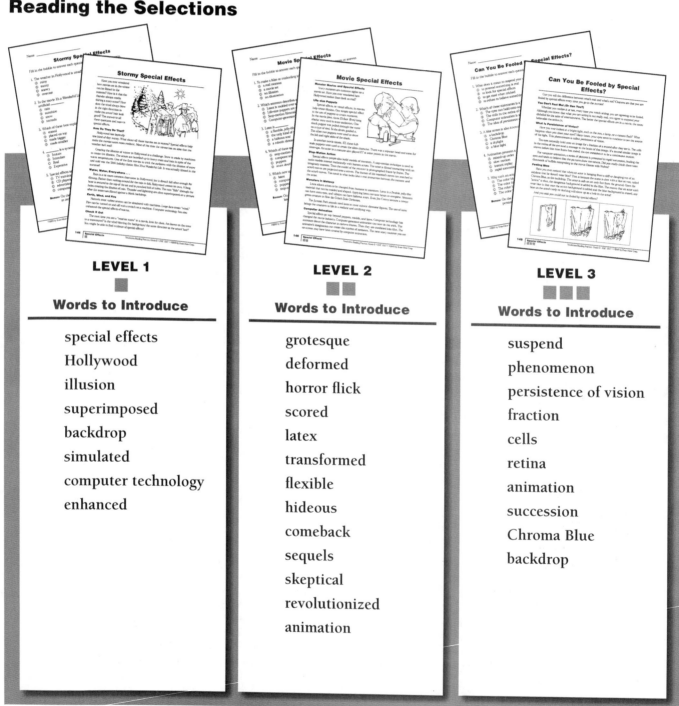

LEVEL 1

Words to Introduce

special effects

Hollywood

illusion

superimposed

backdrop

simulated

computer technology

enhanced

LEVEL 2

Words to Introduce

grotesque

deformed

horror flick

scored

latex

transformed

flexible

hideous

comeback

sequels

skeptical

revolutionized

animation

LEVEL 3

Words to Introduce

suspend

phenomenon

persistence of vision

fraction

cells

retina

animation

succession

Chroma Blue

backdrop

Nonfiction Reading Practice, Grade 6 • EMC 3317 • ©2003 by Evan-Moor Corp.

Special Effects in Movies

Use of Latex

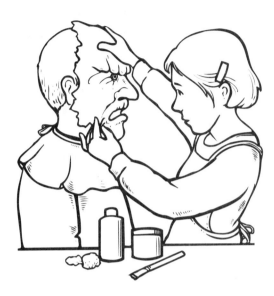

The use of a jelly-like substance called latex has helped create realistic-looking monster masks for actors.

Snow Machine

Large fans blow on the set to simulate high winds. There are machines that can simulate rain, snow, and fire as well.

Computer Animation

Animators draw objects in a comic-strip sequence on computers. Then they are set in motion on-screen.

Compositing

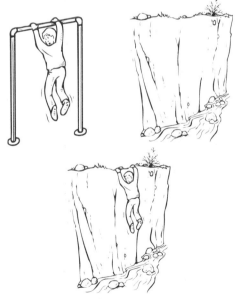

Compositing is a technique that shows one shot superimposed on another, resulting in a composite shot.

Stormy Special Effects

Have you ever wondered how movies set in the winter can be filmed in the summer? How is it that the thunder always cracks during a scary scene? How does the wind always blow in the right direction to make the actors' hair look good? The answer to all these questions and more is special effects.

How Do They Do That?

Hollywood has basically one kind of day: sunny. What about all those movies set in storms? Special effects help make the movies seem more realistic. Most of the time the viewer has no idea that the weather isn't real!

Creating the illusion of winter in Hollywood is a challenge. Snow is made by machines to create the illusion. The actors are bundled up in heavy coats and hats in spite of the warm temperatures. One of the first movies to trick the audience with the illusion of snow and cold was the 1946 holiday classic film *It's a Wonderful Life*. It was actually filmed in the summer!

Water, Water, Everywhere . . .

Rain is a bit more common than snow in Hollywood, but it doesn't fall often enough for filming. Rather than waiting around for the rain to fall, Hollywood creates its own. A long hose is secured to the top of the set and is punched full of holes. The rain "falls" through the holes creating the illusion of rain. Thunder and lightning are often superimposed on a picture after the actors are filmed against a blank backdrop.

Earth, Wind, and Fire

Nature's most violent storms can be simulated with machines. Large fans create "wind." Fire can be turned on and off with a switch on a machine. Computer technology has also enhanced the special effects of storms.

Check It Out

The next time you see a "weather scene" in a movie, look for clues. Are leaves on the trees in a snowstorm? Is the wind blowing the background the same direction as the actors' hair? You might be able to find evidence of special effects!

Nonfiction Reading Practice, Grade 6 • EMC 3317 • ©2003 by Evan-Moor Corp.

Name _____

Stormy Special Effects

Fill in the bubble to answer each question or complete each sentence.

1. The weather in Hollywood is usually _____.
   Ⓐ rainy
   Ⓑ sunny
   Ⓒ snowy
   Ⓓ overcast

2. In the movie *It's a Wonderful Life*, the audience was fooled by artificial _____.
   Ⓐ rain
   Ⓑ sunshine
   Ⓒ snow
   Ⓓ tornado

3. Which of these best explains the term *superimposed*?
   Ⓐ erased
   Ⓑ placed on top
   Ⓒ made bigger
   Ⓓ made smaller

4. _____ is a synonym for the word *simulate*.
   Ⓐ Imitate
   Ⓑ Stimulate
   Ⓒ Real
   Ⓓ Expensive

5. Special effects are often enhanced by _____.
   Ⓐ TV monitors
   Ⓑ CD players
   Ⓒ advertising
   Ⓓ computer technology

Bonus: On the back of this page, list three things you would look for in a movie in order to spot flaws in the weather-related special effects.

Movie Special Effects

Monster Movies and Special Effects

Scary monsters are common sights on a movie set. Have you ever wondered how Hollywood makes them look so real?

Life-size Puppets

Special effects, or visual effects, in movies help create illusion. One simple special effect is the use of puppets to create monsters. In the movie *Jaws*, three 25-foot (8-m) long sharks were used to scare audiences. One shark puppet was pulled through the water on a type of sled. Scuba divers guided it. The other two puppets were used to show the left and right sides of the shark.

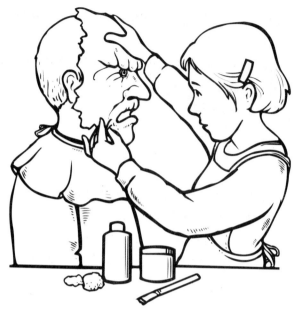

In another movie classic, *ET*, three full-scale puppets were used to create the alien character. There was a separate head and torso for close-ups. An actor in a costume also played ET at some points in the movie.

Stop-Motion Action

Special effects people also build models of monsters. A stop-motion technique is used to make models interact realistically with human actors. The actor is filmed interacting with an imaginary monster. Then the model of the monster is photographed frame by frame. The actor's moves are projected onto a screen. The frames of the monster's moves are matched to the actor's moves. The result is what looks like a real interaction between the monster and the actor.

Monsters in Makeup

Latex allows actors to be changed from humans to monsters. Latex is a flexible, jelly-like material that can be molded and shaped. Applying latex can take hours to complete. Monsters can have extra eyes, and villains can have hideous scars. Even Jim Carrey became a creepy green creature in *How the Grinch Stole Christmas*.

The *Jurassic Park* sequels used latex to cover robotic dinosaur figures. The use of latex brings the creatures to life in a realistic and terrifying way.

Computer Animation

Special effects go way beyond puppets, models, and latex. Computer technology has changed the movie industry. Computer-generated animation can now do the trick. The animator draws the character in cartoon frames. Then they are combined into film. The animator's imagination can create the scariest of monsters. The next scary monster you see on-screen may have been created by computer animation.

Nonfiction Reading Practice, Grade 6 • EMC 3317 • ©2003 by Evan-Moor Corp.

Name _____

Movie Special Effects

Fill in the bubble to answer each question or complete each sentence or answer.

1. To make a false or misleading image in special effects is to create _____.
   - Ⓐ a real monster
   - Ⓑ a movie set
   - Ⓒ an illusion
   - Ⓓ an illustration

2. Which sentence describes a simple technique used in special effects?
   - Ⓐ Latex is molded over an actor's fact to transform him into a monster.
   - Ⓑ Life-size puppets are created to represent monsters.
   - Ⓒ Stop-motion filmmaking shows the actor interacting with the monsters.
   - Ⓓ Computer-generated images are placed into the monster movie.

3. *Latex is* _____.
   - Ⓐ a flexible, jelly-like material
   - Ⓑ the only kind of paint used on the set
   - Ⓒ a hideous scar
   - Ⓓ a robotic dinosaur figure

4. Which of these special effects' methods was <u>not</u> mentioned in the article?
   - Ⓐ stop-motion filming
   - Ⓑ computer animation
   - Ⓒ puppets
   - Ⓓ stunt doubles

5. Which new special effects tool has changed the movie industry?
   - Ⓐ latex
   - Ⓑ computer animation
   - Ⓒ puppetry
   - Ⓓ stop-motion filming

Bonus: On the back of this page, write about a movie you have seen that used latex as a special effect.

Can You Be Fooled by Special Effects?

Can you tell the difference between what's real and what's not? Chances are that you are fooled by special effects every time you go to the movies!

You Can't Fool Me! (Or Can You?)

Whether you realize it or not, every time you watch acting, you are agreeing to be fooled. Although you know that what you are seeing is not really real, you agree to suspend your disbelief for the sake of entertainment. The better the special effects are in a movie, the more believable the action is.

What Is Persistence of Vision?

Have you ever looked at a bright light, such as the sun, a lamp, or a camera flash? What happens when you close your eyes? Many times, your eyes seem to continue to see the source of the light. This phenomenon is called persistence of vision.

The eyes naturally hold onto an image for a fraction of a second after they see it. The cells in the retina of the eye send a message to the brain of that image. If a second similar image is shown before this time frame has ended, the eye considers it to be a continuous motion.

For computer animation, a series of pictures is presented in rapid succession, leading the eyes and brain to believe that the pictures show movement. Did you really think there were thousands of buffalo stampeding in the movie *Dances with Wolves*?

Feeling Blue

Have you ever noticed that when an actor is hanging from a cliff or dangling out of an airplane that he doesn't wear blue? That is because the scene is shot with a blue screen, called Chroma Blue, as the backdrop. The actor is safe on set only feet from the ground. Once the "action" is shot, the dangerous background is added to the film. The reason that an actor can't wear blue is that once the action background is added and the blue background is erased, any blue on the actor's body or clothing will show up as a hole in the actor!

And you said you could not be fooled by special effects?

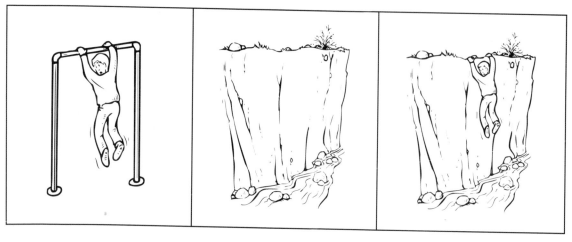

Nonfiction Reading Practice, Grade 6 • EMC 3317 • ©2003 by Evan-Moor Corp.

Name _____

Use your own paper!

Can You Be Fooled by Special Effects?

Fill in the bubble to answer each question or complete each sentence.

1. What does it mean to *suspend your disbelief*?
   - Ⓐ to pretend something is real
   - Ⓑ to look for special effects
   - Ⓒ to get mad when tricked
   - Ⓓ to refuse to believe something is real

2. Which of these statements is a fact about the idea of *persistence of vision*?
   - Ⓐ The eyes can hold onto an image for a minute after they see it.
   - Ⓑ The cells in the retina of the eye send a message to the brain of the image.
   - Ⓒ Computer animation is another name for persistence of vision.
   - Ⓓ The idea of persistence of vision is phenomenal.

3. A *blue screen* is also known as _____.
   - Ⓐ a backdrop
   - Ⓑ Chroma Blue
   - Ⓒ a skylight
   - Ⓓ a blue light

4. Animation presents a series of pictures in _____.
   - Ⓐ mixed-up order
   - Ⓑ slow motion
   - Ⓒ instant replay
   - Ⓓ rapid succession

5. Why can't an actor wear blue to shoot a special effects scene?
   - Ⓐ The color blue shows up as red.
   - Ⓑ The color blue shows up as background color.
   - Ⓒ The color blue shows up as a hole on-screen.
   - Ⓓ The color blue shows up as black.

Bonus: On the back of this page, write a paragraph explaining the concept of persistence of vision. Be sure to include an example of how it is used.

★ **Complete paragraph!**

Drum and Bugle Corps

Introducing the Topic

1. Reproduce page 151 for individual students, or make a transparency to use with a group or the whole class.

2. Ask students how many of them enjoy playing an instrument. Discuss the kinds of instruments that are fun to play and the kinds of venues in which to play them, such as in a band or orchestra. Show students the picture of the four sections of a drum and bugle corps. Share with students that a drum and bugle corps is a marching musical group that plays forward-facing brass instruments and percussion instruments and has a color guard.

Reading the Selections

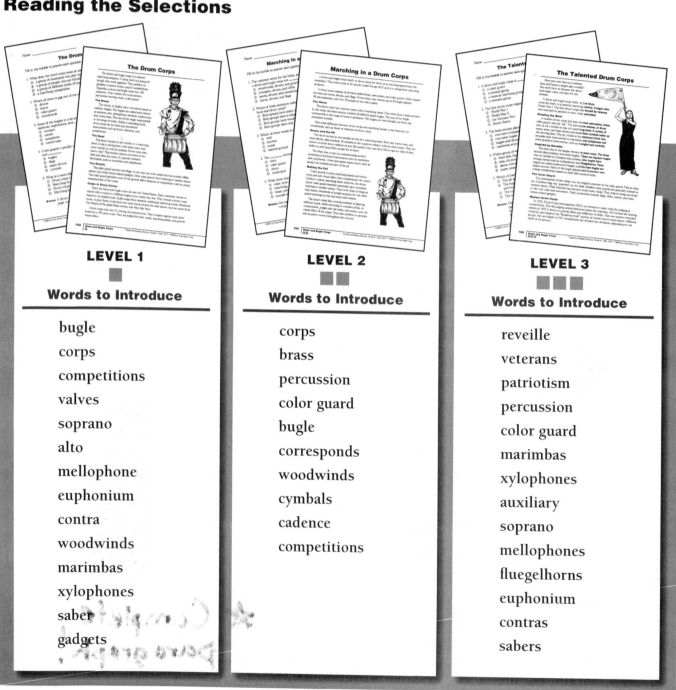

LEVEL 1
Words to Introduce

- bugle
- corps
- competitions
- valves
- soprano
- alto
- mellophone
- euphonium
- contra
- woodwinds
- marimbas
- xylophones
- saber
- gadgets

LEVEL 2
Words to Introduce

- corps
- brass
- percussion
- color guard
- bugle
- corresponds
- woodwinds
- cymbals
- cadence
- competitions

LEVEL 3
Words to Introduce

- reveille
- veterans
- patriotism
- percussion
- color guard
- marimbas
- xylophones
- auxiliary
- soprano
- mellophones
- fluegelhorns
- euphonium
- contras
- sabers

Drum and Bugle Corps

Horn Section

The horn section is the largest section of most drum and bugle corps. Corp members march and play different sized bugles.

Drum Section

Drummers march in precision playing snare, tenor, and bass drums. Sometimes there is a cymbal line, too.

The Pit

The front line is called the pit. This is a nonmarching section at the front the field. Keyboard instruments such as marimbas, xylophones, and chimes are played. Other percussion instruments such as gongs and cymbals are included.

Color Guard

The color guard consists of members who perform using flags, imitation rifles, or other various props.

The Drum Corps

The drum and bugle corps is a musical marching program. A corps (kôr) is a group of people who work together. They perform in parades, at sports events, and in competitions. Typically, a drum and bugle corps has 128 members. They consist of a brass section, a percussion section, and a color guard.

The Brass

The horns, or bugles, have two valves based on military bugles. The bugles are called such names as soprano, alto, mellophone, baritone, euphonuim, and contra bass. The size of the bugle corresponds to the range of notes. Unlike a marching band, drum corps do not have any woodwind instruments, such as flutes, clarinets, and saxophones.

The Beat

The drum section is very similar to a marching band. It has a moving line, with snare, bass, and tenor drums, as well as cymbals. A drum corps also has a "pit." This section stays in the front of the field and does not move. It typically contains keyboards, such as marimbas and xylophones.

The Beauty

The color guard section uses flags. It may also use other props such as wooden rifles, sabers, and other theme-related gadgets. Most color guards have training in modern dance. The color guard provides most of the general effect elements of competition with its visual interpretation of the music.

Corps in Every Corner

There are drum and bugle corps all over the United States. Many members choose to march with a corps in a different region from where they live. They choose a drum corps based on its musical style. Styles range from classical, traditional marching music, Broadway tunes, to jazz. Some corps have even used movie themes for their shows, such as music from *The Wizard of Oz, James Bond* movies, and *West Side Story*.

Many drum corps tour the U.S. during the summertime. They compete against each other based on a 100-point scale. They are judged for their music, marching skills, and general visual effect.

Nonfiction Reading Practice, Grade 6 • EMC 3317 • ©2003 by Evan-Moor Corp.

Name _____

The Drum Corps

Fill in the bubble to answer each question or complete each sentence.

1. What does the word *corps* mean as used in this article?
   - Ⓐ a group of musicians that play together
   - Ⓑ a group of people who are friends
   - Ⓒ a group of different kinds of bugles
   - Ⓓ a marching competition

2. Which of these is <u>not</u> one of the sections of a drum corps?
   - Ⓐ drums
   - Ⓑ horns
   - Ⓒ color guard
   - Ⓓ woodwinds

3. Some of the bugles in a drum corps include soprano, alto, mellophone, baritone, euphonium, and _____.
   - Ⓐ trumpet
   - Ⓑ cornet
   - Ⓒ saxophone
   - Ⓓ contra bass

4. Color guards typically use wooden rifles, sabers, theme-related gadgets, and _____.
   - Ⓐ bugles
   - Ⓑ flags
   - Ⓒ snare drums
   - Ⓓ cymbals

5. What is a main difference between a drum corps and a marching band?
   - Ⓐ Drum corps have a moving drum line.
   - Ⓑ Marching bands do not have a color guard.
   - Ⓒ Drum corps do not have woodwinds.
   - Ⓓ Marching bands use two-valve bugles.

Bonus: A drum and bugle corps typically has 128 members. On the back of this page, write the other main features of a drum and bugle corps.

Marching in a Drum Corps

A drum and bugle corps (kôr), or drum corps for short, is an exciting opportunity for musicians. The junior corps is for people under the age of 21 and is a competitive marching program.

A drum corps consists of sections called brass, percussion, and color guard. Other names for them are horns, drums, and flags. A drum corps may contain up to 60 bugle players, 30 percussionists, and over 30 people in the color guard.

The Horns

The drum corps has common traits with a marching band. They both have a brass section. In the corps, the brass section consists of different sized bugles. The size of the bugle corresponds to the range of notes it produces. The bugles are held straight out from the musicians' mouths.

One main difference between drum corps and marching bands is that there are no woodwinds, such as flutes or clarinets in drum corps.

Drums and the Pit

The drum section is very similar to that of a marching band. Both play snare, bass, and tenor drums, plus cymbals. Drummers in the corps are seldom without their sticks. They are known to break into a cadence on any flat surface they can find. Warm-ups are often 8-beat drills on each hand that can last for an hour.

The front line, or pit, is a nonmarching section consisting of keyboard instruments such as marimbas and xylophones. Other percussion instruments such as gongs and cymbals are part of the pit.

Making the Cut

Color guards in both marching bands and drum corps provide visual effect that complements the music. Unlike a typical marching band, however, the drum corps' color guard members generally have extensive training in modern dance. They twirl rifles or flags as they dance. Hundreds of people audition for the color guard openings in the top corps each season.

The drum corps has a strong tradition of playing difficult music while marching in complex drills. At competitions, judges rate the brass, percussion, and the visual effect of the corps. They also perform in parades and at sports events throughout the country.

Nonfiction Reading Practice, Grade 6 • EMC 3317 • ©2003 by Evan-Moor Corp.

Name _____

Marching in a Drum Corps

Fill in the bubble to answer each question or complete each sentence.

1. The common terms for the brass, percussion, and color guard sections of a drum and bugle corps are _____.
   - Ⓐ woodwinds, drums, and guard
   - Ⓑ trumpets, drums, and rifles
   - Ⓒ horns, drums, and woodwinds
   - Ⓓ horns, drums, and flags

2. Which of these sentences makes a correct comparison between a marching band and drum corps?
   - Ⓐ Both groups have snare, bass, and tenor drums in their drum section.
   - Ⓑ Both groups have a color guard that takes modern dance lessons.
   - Ⓒ Both groups have woodwinds in their groups.
   - Ⓓ Both groups have only bugles in their brass section.

3. Which of these words is a synonym for the word *cadence*?
   - Ⓐ drill
   - Ⓑ rhythm
   - Ⓒ music
   - Ⓓ marching band

4. The _____ section of a drum corps usually has training in modern dance.
   - Ⓐ horn
   - Ⓑ color guard
   - Ⓒ drum
   - Ⓓ woodwind

5. What three things do judges rate at a competition?
   - Ⓐ color, style of music, and complicated drills
   - Ⓑ marching, dancing, and moving in a straight line
   - Ⓒ brass, percussion, and the general visual effect of the corps
   - Ⓓ sounds of the snare drums, cymbals, and bugles

Bonus: On the back of this page, explain how drummers prepare for a drum corps performance.

The Talented Drum Corps

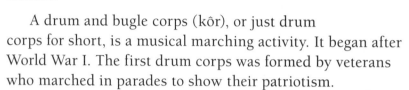

Have you ever been at a military base and heard a bugler play reveille? You don't have to because the drum and bugle corps will play for you instead.

A drum and bugle corps (kôr), or just drum corps for short, is a musical marching activity. It began after World War I. The first drum corps was formed by veterans who marched in parades to show their patriotism.

Keeping the Beat

A modern drum corps has four sections: percussion, brass, color guard, and the "pit." The percussion section, or drum line, is very similar to that of a marching band. A variety of snare, tenor, and bass drums and sometimes cymbals make up the moving lines. The pit, which is the stationary front line, includes such instruments as marimbas and xylophones and other auxiliary instruments, such as triangles and cowbells.

Inspired by Reveille

The horn line is the largest section in most corps. The brass section plays military two-valve bugles. There are soprano bugles that are similar to trumpets and cornets. Alto bugles have strange names such as mellophones and fluegelhorns. Tenor bugles are called euphonium bugles, and the bass bugles are called contras. Many of the bugle players and drummers earn college scholarships based on their elite musical skills.

The Color Guard

The presentation of the colors was the original purpose of the color guard. This is when the American flag was "guarded" on the field. Modern color guards are generally trained in modern dance. Their function has become much more visual. They help to bring the music to life with color and movement. Their accessories include flags, rifles, sabers, and other theme-related gadgets.

Modern Drum Corps

In 1972, Drum Corps International (DCI) was formed to make rules for judging at competitions. The old judging system deducted points for mistakes. DCI revised the scoring system in 1975 to focus on general effect and difficulty of skills. This new system rewarded creativity and inspired the "Broadway-style" aspects of modern drum corps shows. Different groups that participate in DCI competitions are divided into divisions, depending on the skills of the groups.

Name _____

The Talented Drum Corps

Fill in the bubble to answer each question or complete each sentence.

1. A drum and bugle corps is _____.
   - Ⓐ a color guard
   - Ⓑ a musical group
   - Ⓒ a musical marching group
   - Ⓓ a veterans group

2. The first drum corps began after _____.
   - Ⓐ World War I
   - Ⓑ World War II
   - Ⓒ the Vietnam War
   - Ⓓ Desert Storm

3. The brass section plays military _____.
   - Ⓐ two-valve trumpets
   - Ⓑ two-valve bugles
   - Ⓒ bugles and drums
   - Ⓓ marimbas and xylophones

4. Which group of words best describes the drum section of the corps?
   - Ⓐ front line, horn line, and pit
   - Ⓑ beat, rhythm, and melody
   - Ⓒ dance, movement, and color
   - Ⓓ snare, tenor, bass, and cymbals

5. Which of these statements is true about the drum and bugle corps?
   - Ⓐ The pit is the stationary percussion section that makes up the front line.
   - Ⓑ The bugle corps is made up of three sections: brass, percussion, and bugles.
   - Ⓒ The color guard's purpose is to maintain order.
   - Ⓓ The modern judging system focuses on deducting points for mistakes.

Bonus: Choose one of the unusual-sounding instruments. On the back of this page, draw what you think it looks like and describe what kinds of sounds it makes. If possible, look up the instrument on the Internet or in a music book to see if you had the right idea.

Frank Lloyd Wright

Introducing the Topic

1. Reproduce page 159 for individual students, or make a transparency to use with a group or the whole class.

2. Share with students that they will read about a famous architect who designed over 1,000 homes and public buildings that had an "organic" feel to them. Ask students what is meant by *organic* (harmonizing with nature). Read and discuss with students the time line of Frank Lloyd Wright's life. Tell students the emphasis of the time line is more on his architectural life than a personal one.

Reading the Selections

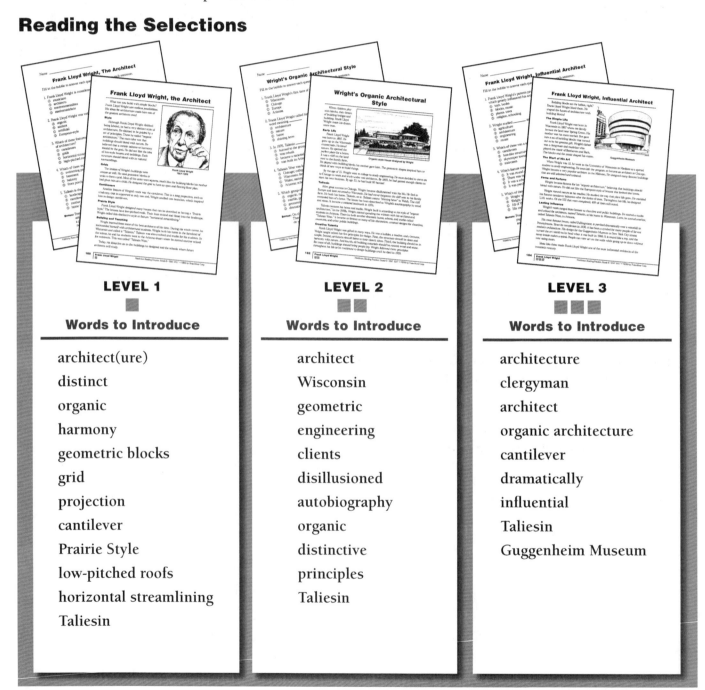

LEVEL 1
■
Words to Introduce

architect(ure)

distinct

organic

harmony

geometric blocks

grid

projection

cantilever

Prairie Style

low-pitched roofs

horizontal streamlining

Taliesin

LEVEL 2
■ ■
Words to Introduce

architect

Wisconsin

geometric

engineering

clients

disillusioned

autobiography

organic

distinctive

principles

Taliesin

LEVEL 3
■ ■ ■
Words to Introduce

architecture

clergyman

architect

organic architecture

cantilever

dramatically

influential

Taliesin

Guggenheim Museum

Nonfiction Reading Practice, Grade 6 • EMC 3317 • ©2003 by Evan-Moor Corp.

Time Line of Frank Lloyd Wright's Life

1867 — Born in Richland Center, Wisconsin.

1882 — Attended the University of Wisconsin to study engineering.

1887 — Moved to Chicago to study architecture.

1900 — By this time, had designed 60 homes.

1911 — Built his home, called Taliesin, in Wisconsin.

1916 — Designed the Imperial Hotel in Tokyo, Japan.

1936 — Designed Fallingwater home that was built over a waterfall.

1938 — Built Taliesin West, his winter home and architectural school in Arizona.

1955 — Designed the Guggenheim Museum, which was completed after his death.

1959 — Died on April 9 in Arizona.

Wright designed 1,141 works over his lifetime.

Frank Lloyd Wright, the Architect

What can you build with simple blocks? Frank Lloyd Wright saw endless possibilities. His ideas for architecture made him one of the greatest architects ever!

Style

Although Frank Lloyd Wright disliked being labeled, he had a very distinct style of architecture. He claimed to be guided by a set of principles. These he called "organic architecture." The main idea was that buildings should blend with nature. He believed that a certain balance or harmony should be the goal. He did not like the idea of box-style houses and buildings. Each structure should blend with its natural surroundings.

Frank Lloyd Wright
1867–1959

Grids

The insides of Wright's buildings were unique as well. He used geometric blocks or units to form a grid. Most of the units were squares, much like the building blocks his mother had given him as a child. He designed the grid to have an open and flowing floor plan.

Cantilevers

Another feature of Wright's work was the cantilever. This is a long projection, such as a balcony, that is supported at only one end. Wright studied tree branches, which inspired him to design cantilevers.

Prairie Style

Frank Lloyd Wright designed many houses that can be described as having a "Prairie Style." The houses have low-pitched roofs. Their lines extend and blend into the landscape. Wright called this distinctive style or feature "horizontal streamlining."

Building and Teaching

Wright learned from some of the best architects of his time. During his whole career, he surrounded himself with architectural students. Wright built his home in the farmland of Wisconsin and called it "Taliesin." Taliesin was also a school and studio for his students. In the winter, he and his students went to the Arizona desert where he started another school for architects. This was called "Taliesin West."

Today, his ideas live on in the buildings he designed and the schools where future architects still study.

Nonfiction Reading Practice, Grade 6 • EMC 3317 • ©2003 by Evan-Moor Corp.

Name _____

Frank Lloyd Wright, the Architect

Fill in the bubble to answer each question or complete each sentence.

1. Frank Lloyd Wright is considered to be one of the greatest _____ ever.
   - Ⓐ musicians
   - Ⓑ architects
   - Ⓒ environmentalists
   - Ⓓ mathematicians

2. Frank Lloyd Wright was well known for his _____ architecture.
   - Ⓐ organic
   - Ⓑ ancient
   - Ⓒ artificial
   - Ⓓ European-style

3. Which of these features is <u>not</u> usually associated with Wright's style of architecture?
   - Ⓐ cantilevers
   - Ⓑ grids
   - Ⓒ horizontal streamlining
   - Ⓓ high-pitched roofs

4. Which of these words is an example of a *cantilever*?
   - Ⓐ swimming pool
   - Ⓑ basement
   - Ⓒ balcony
   - Ⓓ front porch

5. *Taliesin* is the name of Frank Lloyd Wright's _____.
   - Ⓐ landscape design
   - Ⓑ cantilever design
   - Ⓒ mother
   - Ⓓ home in Wisconsin

Bonus: Pretend you are one of Wright's architectural students. You have been asked to design a new home for Wright. On the back of this page, draw a picture of a home Wright would like to live in. Include a name for his new home.

Wright's Organic Architectural Style

When children play with blocks, they dream of building bridges and building. Frank Lloyd Wright made his dream come true.

Early Life

Frank Lloyd Wright was born in 1867. He grew up in the Wisconsin countryside. He loved nature. He spotted the perfect place for a home. It was a cliff on the land next to the family farm.

Organic style house designed by Wright

He played with building blocks his mother gave him. The geometric shapes inspired him to think of new ways to build things.

By the age of 15, Wright went to college to study engineering. He soon decided to move on to Chicago to work and study under real architects. By 1893, he had gained enough clients to start his own business. By age 33, he had built 60 homes!

Taliesin

After great success in Chicago, Wright became disillusioned with his life. He fled to Europe and later returned to Wisconsin. He had never forgotten the cliff next to his family farm. He built his home, Taliesin, on it. *Taliesin* means "shining brow" in Welsh. The cliff reminded him of a brow. The house has been described as Wright's autobiography in wood and stone. It became a national landmark in 1976.

Taliesin became his home and studio. Wright built it according to his style of "organic architecture." In the 1930s, Wright started spending the winters with his architectural students in Arizona. There he built another dramatic home, school, and studio called "Taliesin West." It became as famous as many of his distinctive, unusual designs for churches, museums, and other public buildings.

Creative Talents

Frank Lloyd Wright was gifted in many ways. He was a builder, a teacher, and a lecturer. Wright taught others his five principles for design. First, the structure should be clean and simple. Second, architects should listen to their client's ideas. Third, the building should be in harmony with nature. And fourth, all building materials should be natural wood and stone. But most of all, buildings should bring people joy. Wright followed these principles throughout his life as he continued to design buildings until he died in 1959.

Nonfiction Reading Practice, Grade 6 • EMC 3317 • ©2003 by Evan-Moor Corp.

Name _____

Wright's Organic Architectural Style

Fill in the bubble to answer each question or complete each sentence.

1. Frank Lloyd Wright's first taste of success was in _____.
   - Ⓐ Wisconsin
   - Ⓑ Chicago
   - Ⓒ Europe
   - Ⓓ Arizona

2. Frank Lloyd Wright called his home Taliesin. The word *Taliesin* is a Welsh word meaning _____.
   - Ⓐ architecture
   - Ⓑ nature
   - Ⓒ home
   - Ⓓ shining brow

3. In 1976, Taliesin _____.
   - Ⓐ burned to the ground
   - Ⓑ was rebuilt
   - Ⓒ became a national landmark
   - Ⓓ was built in Arizona

4. Taliesin West was located in _____ and was a home, studio, and _____.
   - Ⓐ Chicago; college
   - Ⓑ Wisconsin; farm
   - Ⓒ Wales; national landmark
   - Ⓓ Arizona; school

5. Which group of words best describes Wright's architectural style?
   - Ⓐ organic, natural, simple
   - Ⓑ marble, grand, and complex
   - Ⓒ geometric, square, and artificial
   - Ⓓ dramatic, unusual, and ornate

Bonus: On the back of this page, explain Frank Lloyd's five principles of design. Then answer the following question: Of the five principles, which one do you think is the most important?

Frank Lloyd Wright, Influential Architect

Building blocks are for babies, right? Frank Lloyd Wright liked them. He shaped the future of architecture with building blocks!

The Simple Life

Frank Lloyd Wright was born in Wisconsin in 1867 where his family farmed the land near Spring Green. His mother was his main teacher. She gave him a set of building blocks that turned out to be his greatest gift. Wright's father was a clergyman and musician who played the music of Beethoven and Bach. The blocks and the music shaped his vision.

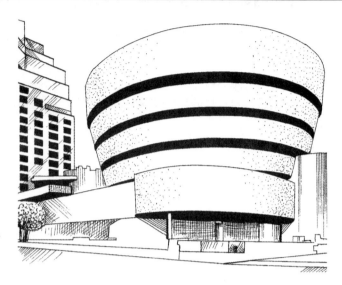

Guggenheim Museum

The Start of His Art

When Wright was 15, he went to the University of Wisconsin in Madison as a special student to study engineering. He soon left the program to become an architect in Chicago. Wright became a very popular architect in the Midwest. He designed many famous buildings that are still admired and imitated.

Fame and Fortune

Wright became famous for his "organic architecture," believing that buildings should blend with nature. He did not like the European style of houses that looked like boxes.

Wright viewed nature as his teacher. He studied the way that plant life grew. He modeled his famous cantilever balconies after the limbs of trees. Throughout his life, he designed 1,141 works. Of the 532 that were completed, 409 of them still stand.

Lasting Influence

Wright's work ranged from houses to churches and public buildings. He started a studio and school for architects, named Taliesin, at his home in Wisconsin. Later, he started another, called Taliesin West, in Arizona.

His most famous house, called Fallingwater, is perched dramatically over a waterfall in Pennsylvania. Since its completion in 1936, it has been a symbol for many people of far-out modern architecture. His design for the Guggenheim Museum in New York City almost turned the art world on its head when it was built in 1960. It is round like a top, and the ramp inside makes a spiral. People can view art on the walls while going up or down without ever using stairs.

Ideas like these made Frank Lloyd Wright one of the most influential architects of the twentieth century.

Name _____

Frank Lloyd Wright, Influential Architect

Fill in the bubble to answer each question or complete each sentence.

1. Frank Lloyd Wright's parents provided him with _____ and _____, which greatly influenced his architectural vision.
   - Ⓐ toys, books
   - Ⓑ blocks, music
   - Ⓒ plants, trees
   - Ⓓ religion, schooling

2. Wright studied _____ at the University of Wisconsin.
   - Ⓐ agriculture
   - Ⓑ architecture
   - Ⓒ engineering
   - Ⓓ music

3. Which of these was a significant feature of Wright's buildings?
   - Ⓐ cantilevers
   - Ⓑ box-like structures
   - Ⓒ skyscraper towers
   - Ⓓ staircases

4. Which feature made Fallingwater a symbol of far-out design?
   - Ⓐ It was round and had a spiral ramp.
   - Ⓑ There was no running water in the house.
   - Ⓒ It was a school and studio for experimental architects.
   - Ⓓ It was perched over a waterfall.

5. Which of these statements is true about Wright's designs?
   - Ⓐ Wright was greatly influenced by European style.
   - Ⓑ Wright was famous for his organic architecture.
   - Ⓒ All of Wright's designs were far-out, and people scorned them.
   - Ⓓ His most famous house was called Guggenheim.

Bonus: Pretend the Guggenheim Museum has just opened. On the back of this page, write a review for an architectural magazine telling your thoughts and opinions on its design.

Note: This page may be reproduced for student use.

Name _____

Write the important details of the famous person's life.

Who _____

Where _____

Sketch

Where (he/she lives or lived)

_____

_____

_____

_____

_____

_____

What (he/she does or did)

_____

_____

_____

_____

_____

_____

_____

Why (it is important to know about him/her)

_____

_____

_____

_____

_____

_____

Name _____

KWL Chart

Before reading the article, write what you already know about the topic. Write what you want to know about the topic. After you finish reading the article, write what you learned about the topic.

Topic:		
K What I **K**now	**W** What I **W**ant to Know	**L** What I **L**earned

Name _____

Making an Outline

As you read the article, take notes on three important main ideas or subtopics. After you have read the article, write the title of the article. Write three subtopics as main headings (I–III) in the outline. Write each subtopic's details (A–C) in the outline.

_____

Title of article

I. _____

   A. _____

   B. _____

   C. _____

II. _____

   A. _____

   B. _____

   C. _____

III. _____

   A. _____

   B. _____

   C. _____

Name _____

Multisection Web

Use this web to write the main idea and supporting details for three important paragraphs in the article.

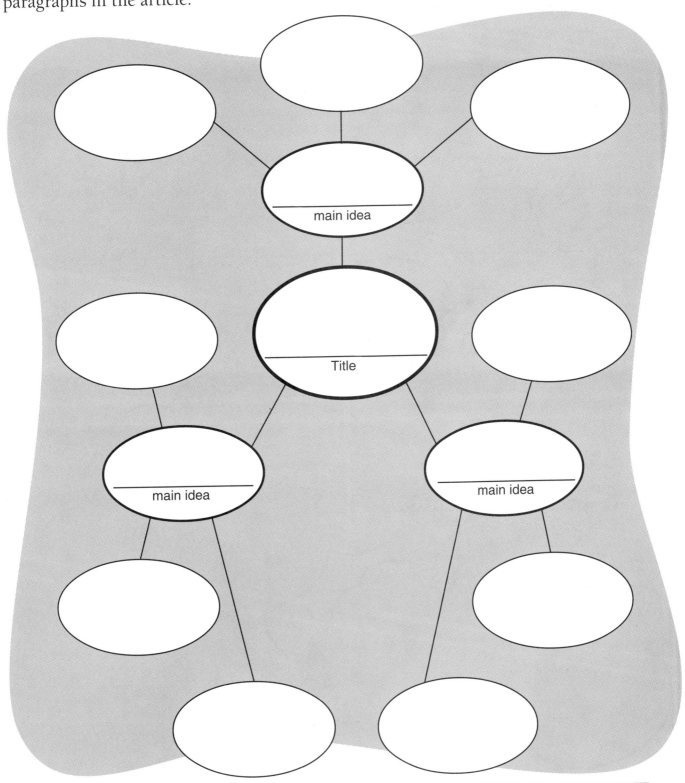

Name _____

Sequence Chart

Use this chart to sequence the events in the article.

Nonfiction Reading Practice, Grade 6 • EMC 3317 • ©2003 by Evan-Moor Corp.

Name _____

Vocabulary Quilt

As you read the article, write new words and their meanings in the quilt squares.

Answer Key

Nonfiction Reading Practice, Grade 6 • EMC 3317 • ©2003 by Evan-Moor Corp.

page 9
1. D
2. C
3. B
4. A
5. B
Bonus: Answers will vary, but should include a drawing and caption. Possible facts for the caption might include size, location, or features.

page 11
1. C
2. D
3. A
4. A
5. B
Bonus: Answers will vary, but the postcard should include a salutation, body of facts, and a closing. An address and picture should also be included.

page 13
1. B
2. D
3. C
4. A
5. C
Bonus: Answers will vary, but should define timeless wonder. A possible answer might be that it is a monument that has lasted for a long time.

page 17
1. B
2. C
3. D
4. A
5. C
Bonus: Answers will vary, but should reference a choice and three reasons. An example might be: I would like to be a defense lawyer so I can prove a person is innocent. I would like to find witnesses and figure out the facts.

page 19
1. A
2. D
3. C
4. C
5. B
Bonus: Answers should include the following steps: The lawyer presents a case to a panel of judges. The panel makes a ruling. If one of the lawyers thinks a legal error was made in appellate court, an appeal may be made to the Supreme Court.

page 21
1. C
2. D
3. A
4. D
5. B

Bonus: Answers should reference that the court system is a protector of the rights and freedoms of citizens.

page 25
1. C
2. A
3. C
4. C
5. D
Bonus: Answers will vary, but should reference three accomplishments such as: increased trade, repaired temples, mined for ores, and brought peace for 20 years.

page 27
1. A
2. C
3. A
4. B
5. D
Bonus: Answers will vary. A possible answer might be that Egyptian laws did not allow women the same rights as men, and Hatshepsut wanted to show she had the power of a man.

page 29
1. B
2. A
3. B
4. D
5. C
Bonus: Answers will vary. One possible answer might be that Hatshepsut may have been murdered since Thutmose III ordered all her images and references to her destroyed.

page 33
1. C
2. D
3. B
4. C
5. D
Bonus: Answers should reference events on each of the 5 days. **Day 1:** ceremonies and feasts honoring Zeus. **Day 2:** footraces, long jumps, and chariot racing. **Day 3:** a parade. **Day 4:** discus and javelin throwing, boxing and wrestling matches. **Day 5:** winners received laurel wreaths.

page 35
1. D
2. C
3. B
4. C
5. A
Bonus: Answers will vary. A possible choice might be the stade. Three reasons might include the joy of running for 200 yards (180 m), the idea of competing alone rather than as a team, and that the stade was less dangerous than the others.

page 37
1. B
2. D
3. D
4. C
5. C

Bonus: Answers will vary. Possible reasons might include: a thrill of danger, fast-paced, and exciting to watch something few attempt.

page 41
1. B
2. D
3. A
4. B
5. C

Bonus: Answers will vary, but possible questions might include: What was it like to be at the top of the world? What or who inspired you to become such a great athlete? What other things would you like to do now that you have climbed all the highest peaks in the world?

page 43
1. A
2. C
3. B
4. D
5. A

Bonus: Answers will vary, but possible challenges might include: Mt. Everest is at 29,035 feet (8,850 m). Icy winds blow at 100 mph (160 km/h) and oxygen levels are low. Weihenmayer's challenges were greater because he was blind.

page 45
1. A
2. D
3. D
4. B
5. C

Bonus: Answers will vary, but should reference the idea that Erik Weihenmayer's blindness did not stop him from enjoying adventure and becoming an expert climber.

page 49
1. D
2. C
3. B
4. C
5. B

Bonus: Answers will vary, but the diagram should include a dolphin with "sound waves" or arrows going toward fish. The sound waves then bounce back to the dolphin. The illustration on page 48 will help.

page 51
1. A
2. C
3. D
4. A
5. B

Bonus: Answers will vary, but should include the following ideas: Vibration is a continuous, very fast, backward and forward movement. Frequency is the number of vibrations per second. Hertz is the basic unit of frequency (equal to one cycle per second). Ultrasound is sound with frequencies higher than 20,000 hertz. Echolocation is navigation using echoes from high-pitched sounds.

page 53
1. A
2. C
3. B
4. D
5. B

Bonus: Answers will vary, but should reference one opinion. An example of an answer might be: I take the side of the environmentalists. Whales have been around for thousands of years. Migration is a natural instinct for whales. With all the computer technology available today, the navy could find alternative ways to watch the borders. One solution may be for the navy to "turn down" the frequency of the sonar instruments below a whale's frequency levels. They could still find objects in the water without upsetting the whales' echolocation system.

page 57
1. D
2. A
3. B
4. C
5. A

Bonus: Answers will vary, but should reference that female manatees teach their calves how to breathe and how to migrate to warmer waters.

page 59
1. D
2. C
3. B
4. A
5. C

Bonus: Answers will vary, but should reference the fact that manatees must migrate to survive. They need warm waters, so Florida manatees leave Florida at colder times and head for the Gulf of Mexico.

page 61
1. D
2. D
3. B
4. C
5. A

Bonus: Answers will vary, but should reference one or more of the following: obey boating speed limits, cut down on waste, not pollute the waters, or join the Save the Manatee Club.

page 65
1. C
2. D
3. B
4. D
5. A
Bonus: Answers will vary, but should reference the fact that Ground Control and the crew worked together to bring the astronauts back to Earth safely.

page 67
1. D
2. A
3. C
4. D
5. B
Bonus: Answers will vary, but possible moments might include: when the crew heard the explosion, when they realized they were running out of oxygen, making their way through the tunnel, or when they realized they were floating in space with no way home.

page 69
1. B
2. C
3. A
4. D
5. C
Bonus: Answers will vary, but should reference the failure was that the astronauts did not accomplish the mission of landing on the moon, but that they were successful in getting the crew back to Earth safely.

page 73
1. C
2. D
3. A
4. B
5. C
Bonus: Answers should reference such measurements as: ISS will be 356 feet (109 m) wide and 290 feet (88 m) long when finished. Solar panels will cover an acre (.4 ha) and ISS will weigh one million pounds (450,000 kg).

page 75
1. B
2. A
3. D
4. D
5. C
Bonus: Answers will vary, but should reference one or more of the following: More protein crystals can be grown in space. Low gravity provides a way to study how body systems react. Creating metal alloys is easier in low gravity conditions.

page 77
1. A
2. C
3. C
4. B
5. D

Bonus: Answers will vary. Advantages might include: More people are given the chance to be in space. It is a possible alternative for overcrowded Earth. Money from private citizens and companies could help pay for scientific space programs. Disadvantages might include: Only the rich could afford it. The more people in space, the more polluted it becomes. Private hotels would replace serious scientific research.

page 81
1. C
2. B
3. B
4. A
5. D
Bonus: Answers will vary, but might reference that the word *silent* refers to the fact that pollution destroys, thus silencing life. The word *Spring* refers to rebirth or nature.

page 83
1. C
2. D
3. D
4. C
5. B
Bonus: Answers will vary. Possible poems might include acrostic, free verse, haiku, or countless others. Students should incorporate words such as: nature, environment, *Silent Spring*, and her name.

page 85
1. C
2. A
3. D
4. B
5. A
Bonus: Answers will vary, but should reference her contributions such as: Her book *Silent Spring* was eye-opening. Because of her efforts, DDT was banned and new laws and regulations were put into place to save the environment.

page 89
1. C
2. C
3. A
4. A
5. B
Bonus: Answers will vary, but five possible things might include: family support, support of friends, not smoking in front of the person trying to quit, getting rid of ashtrays or other reminders, and taking medication to quit.

page 91
1. C
2. D
3. B
4. A
5. C

Bonus: Answers will vary, but the ad should be truthful and be the opposite of what cigarette ads usually look like (young beautiful, athletic, popular people). Ad should include such facts as: average age of a new smoker is 13; 3,000 kids start smoking every day; or that most kids won't date people who smoke.

page 93
1. B
2. A
3. C
4. C
5. D
Bonus: Answers will vary, but possible reasons might include: It is a way of fitting in or belonging to a group. Some kids think it looks cool and are influenced by favorite celebrities in videos or in movies. Or they may like the dangerous thrill of smoking.

page 97
1. C
2. A
3. C
4. D
5. B
Bonus: Answers will vary, but possible rules may be: Don't give out personal information. Tell parents when they are online, or they shouldn't believe everything they read or see online.

page 99
1. C
2. D
3. B
4. A
5. B
Bonus: Answers will vary, but might include: E-mailing family and friends, researching a topic for school, playing games or music, or visiting a virtual museum are all good ways to use the Internet.

page 101
1. B
2. C
3. A
4. B
5. D
Bonus: Answers will vary, but three facts might include: Don't give out personal information. Don't believe everything you read. And don't meet people in chat rooms.

page 105
1. B
2. D
3. C
4. B
5. A

Bonus: Answers will vary, but should reference three things such as: It's a balanced program of muscle toning, stretching, and breathing exercises. They should be done slowly and smoothing. An example for the second answer might be: It is a good exercise program because it helps build strength, balance, and a good posture.

page 107
1. D
2. B
3. A
4. C
5. D
Bonus: Answers should reference that Pilates invented a simple machine to help wounded soldiers in WWI who were bedridden.

page 109
1. B
2. D
3. A
4. B
5. C
Bonus: Answers will vary, but might include: People who are tired of aerobics and weight training are opting for slow, smooth exercises that develop strong, lean muscles.

page 113
1. A
2. B
3. D
4. A
5. C
Bonus: Answers will vary, but should reference one or more of the following ideas: They can work together on money policies. They can control interest rates better. People who travel from one country to another in Western Europe won't have to exchange currency.

page 115
1. C
2. A
3. A
4. D
5. B
Bonus: Answers will vary, but should reference likes and differences between the two currencies. One example of how they are alike is that both have paper bills and metal coins. One example of how they are different is in the denominations of the bills and coins.

page 117
1. D
2. A
3. C
4. B
5. D

Bonus: Answers will vary, but should reference that Sorenson asked people to send him their old currencies before they lost value. He sent the money to a bank in Europe before the deadline. All of it was exchanged for euros. He sent the money to the Kids First Fund, which helps abused children.

page 121
1. C
2. D
3. A
4. B
5. D

Bonus: Answers should reference the idea that young people have more time to put their money into long-term investments.

page 123
1. B
2. D
3. A
4. D
5. C

Bonus: Answers should reference that stocks are not guaranteed and are more risky.

page 125
1. B
2. A
3. C
4. D
5. A

Bonus: Answers will vary. A possible answer might include: I would choose to play the stock market. I am young so I want to have a long-term investment. The risks are great, but I could make a lot of money if I do my research and invest in the right companies.

page 129
1. D
2. A
3. B
4. A
5. C

Bonus: Answers should be: In Iowa, it is 4:00 P.M. and in South Carolina is it 5:00 P.M. Clockfaces should reflect the correct times.

page 131
1. B
2. A
3. C
4. A
5. C

Bonus: Answers should reference the idea that as people cross the International Date Line they either gain or lose a day. For every time zone they cross, the time changes by one hour.

page 133
1. A
2. C
3. C
4. B
5. D

Bonus: Answers will vary. Possible examples might be: **1.** If it is 3:00 P.M. in civilian time, what time is it in Military Time? Answer: 3:00 + 12 = 1500 hours **2.** If it is 1000 hours, what time is it in Standard Time? Answer: 1000 = 10:00 A.M. **3.** If it is 12:00 in 24-Hour Time, what time is it in Military Time? Answer: 2400 hours.

page 137
1. A
2. C
3. B
4. D
5. B

Bonus: Answers will vary. A possible answer might be: I play the piano in a jazz band. I like it when I get to play a solo during the performance. I especially like to play the melody, but I can improvise a little, too. Sometimes I play the electronic piano to get a fuller sound.

page 139
1. A
2. B
3. B
4. D
5. D

Bonus: Answers will vary. A possible answer might be: My favorite period of jazz is the 1930s. That was a time when swing or the big band sound was popular. I like to dance so I would enjoy swing music. Hearing famous singers like Billie Holiday and Nat King Cole would be exciting.

page 141
1. A
2. B
3. C
4. B
5. D

Bonus: Answers will vary, but should reference the idea that people of different races and from different nations contributed to jazz. Jazz brought people together and racial tolerance was apparent.

page 145
1. B
2. C
3. B
4. A
5. D

Bonus: Answers will vary. Three things might include such things as: It's snowing, but car windows are wide open. The wind is blowing, but objects aren't being thrown about. It's raining, but the actor's hair is dry.